GLOBAL STUDIES

VISIONS *for the* GLOBAL ECONOMY

Economic Growth, Global Economic Governance, and Political Economy

JOHN R. GAGAIN JR.

FUNGLODE
FUNDACIÓN GLOBAL
DEMOCRACIA Y DESARROLLO

iUniverse, Inc.
Bloomington

Visions for the Global Economy
Economic Growth, Global Economic Governance, and Political Economy

Copyright © 2012 by John R. Gagain Jr.

All rights reserved. No part of this book may be used or reproduced by any means, graphic, electronic, or mechanical, including photocopying, recording, taping or by any information storage retrieval system without the written permission of the publisher except in the case of brief quotations embodied in critical articles and reviews.

iUniverse books may be ordered through booksellers or by contacting:

iUniverse
1663 Liberty Drive
Bloomington, IN 47403
www.iuniverse.com
1-800-Authors (1-800-288-4677)

Because of the dynamic nature of the Internet, any web addresses or links contained in this book may have changed since publication and may no longer be valid. The views expressed in this work are solely those of the author and do not necessarily reflect the views of the publisher, and the publisher hereby disclaims any responsibility for them.

Any people depicted in stock imagery provided by Thinkstock are models, and such images are being used for illustrative purposes only.
Certain stock imagery © Thinkstock.

Gagain Jr., John R. Visions for the Global Economy: Economic Growth, Global Economic Governance & Political Economy / John R. Gagain Jr. – First Edition – Santo Domingo: Fundación Global Democracia y Desarrollo – FUNGLODE, 2012.
180 p.

ISBN: 978-1-4759-3791-6 (sc)
ISBN: 978-1-4759-3792-3 (hc)
ISBN: 978-1-4759-3793-0 (e)

Library of Congress Control Number: 2012912546

@ Ediciones Funglode, Fundación Global Democracia y Desarrollo Calle Capitán Eugenio de Marchena 26, La Esperilla, Santo Domingo República Dominicana, www.funglode.org

Printed in the United States of America

iUniverse rev. date: 08/01/2012

Dedication

I would like to dedicate this book to the people of the Dominican Republic, especially two of its citizens: John Raymond and Eric John. May their energy and lively spirits always continue to motivate me and give me reason to work tirelessly with them, and for them, in favor of an increasingly better future and better place to live.

Now and forever, will I offer my deepest appreciation to, and admiration for, Dr. Leonel Fernandez—who, like a second father and professor, has taught me so much as I have observed, up close and from afar, every careful measure he has taken as a leader in favor of his peoples' best human interests.

Thank you Vivian for all of your support and sacrifice.

Thank you colleagues and friends at FUNGLODE, COPDES, and the School of International and Public Affairs (SIPA), Columbia University.

CONTENTS

Introduction. ix

PART I: Economic Growth. 1

1) Problems of Economic Growth in Latin America 3
2) The Challenges of Peace and Economic Growth in
   Colombia 35

PART II: Global Economic Governance. 47

3) The Globalization of Citizen-to-Citizen based Growth. . . . 49
4) G7, G8, G20 and the G193: The Proliferation of the
   "Gs" as a Means for Dealing with the Challenges Facing
   the World Economy 55
5) Bridging the Economic and Social Dimensions of
   Global Governance 61
6) The Paradox of Applying National Regulations to a
   Global Market: A Review of Commodity Futures 67
7) The Political Economy of the Eurozone: Global
   Governance's Growing Pains 93
8) The World Outgrows Kyoto: A 20th Century Agreement
   in a 21st Century World: How to Make Climate Stability
   Work for the Global Public Good 109
9) Seoul to Cannes: The Evolution of a G20 and a G-Zero . . 127

PART III: Political Economy 139

10) A Review of Inter-American Relations since the Beginning of the Cold War: A Comparative Perspective from Juan Bosch to CELAC 141

INTRODUCTION

I have been studying Global Studies for a long time. I began in the mid-1990s as an undergraduate student at Pace University in New York, studying International Relations under the tutelage of Dr. Greg Julian. He introduced me to an internship at the United Nations in New York City, students from various countries around the world that participated in his Model United Nations program, as well as the public advocacy agenda of the UN Association of the USA. Since then, I became fascinated with the world, cultures, and languages. I learned about the importance of globalization and the world economy. I learned that global issues entail managing and tracking an enormous amount of constantly changing information. I also learned that there are a select group of global issues that you must know well, especially if you are going to consider yourself a meaningful actor in this increasingly interdependent world. This experience helped me to later serve on official country delegations to annual UN General Assembly sessions in September as well as important World Summits and Conferences as advisor to the President of the Dominican Republic and other world leaders.

This book, Visions for the Global Economy, includes a series of chapters that cover a collection of global issues that I believe every good student of the world must master. In Dr. Julian's classes we always utilized the Internet for our Model UN research. More than sixteen years later, I am sure the role the Internet plays in Model UN research has only grown. I only hope that the Internet has not replaced textbooks.

I never thought I would be hearing myself say that, particularly because I remember back then when Dr. Julian would argue with his Dean in the Social Sciences Department over the power of the Internet as a pedagogical tool vis-à-vis books. Those were the early days of the Internet's inception, and the Dean, an older fellow, favored textbooks; while Dr. Julian and I championed the newfound Internet. In retrospect, I think there is still an important role for the "academic style" textbook.

Visions for the Global Economy may not be considered a class textbook. At least I did not start to write it with that purpose. I did write it, however, with the aim of compiling a series of themes I consider important for Global Studies; and constructing them in a unique way, which I believe will help the reader to effectively learn pivotal issues, accompanied by their foundational aspects— which together present a tool that enables the reader to acquire enough information to be able to go out and debate these very same issues.

A book such as Visions for the Global Economy never existed when I was a student of Model United Nations. I wish there was a book like it that I could have used to supplement my research, however, the only textbook I could remember having was the famous Global Agenda, produced by the UN Association of the USA in New York City, an organization where I later spent three years as Education Coordinator in the late 1990s. The Global Agenda, as an annual publication, provided students with information on the items before the UN General Assembly for that specific year. It was an insightful book, which was discontinued for some years, but has recently made a comeback thanks to the UN Foundation.

Visions for the Global Economy on the other hand provides three things. First, it not only addresses key topics on the global stage, it also addresses them at their core—meaning each chapter of this book aims to take you through the storyline of each issue. Essentially, this is done because students almost always ask the famous question "but why?" after reading. Events and decisions made in world politics and global economic governance always happen because of a reason (or set of reasons); and as a student myself, I would always remember asking, "why would France say that" or "why would the US go there and do that". Global issues, and the decisions world leaders make, are complex; and there never is one clear reason as to why something exists or why something takes place.

Every chapter of this book is written with the intention of finding the foundation or structural aspects of the global issues being addressed in order to help the reader understand "why". For example, Chapter seven entitled "The Paradox of Applying National Regulations to a Global Market: A Review of Commodity Futures" outlines "foundational aspects" such as the various laws and decisions formulated over the course of several decades, which today result in the highly global financial derivatives industry.

Second, Visions for the Global Economy addresses "the arguments". I enjoy arguing contentious global issues, not merely for the sake of being polemic; but rather because I believe we are all compelled, especially in a democratic society, to defend our interests vis-à-vis those of our neighbors. To be a good citizen, you must be civically active. You must know what is going on in your society and community and you must learn the opinions of others while simultaneously putting forth and debating your own ideas and opinions in order to be a good citizen and active contributor to your community's democratic values.

More importantly, there is always another opinion. It is important to put forth your own arguments, but it is just as important, if not more so, to be curious and ask about the other side of the coin. What is the other side of the argument? If more global decision makers were more concerned about learning the flip side of the argument, the world would be a different place today. Every chapter of Visions for the Global Economy is written with the intention of outlining as many sides of the argument as possible. As a student of social science it may not be so hard to develop your own opinions. The trick is learning and understanding different opinions, especially contrasting opinions. This is a task that only the masters of diplomacy conquer.

Finally, every chapter of this book aims to address a key turning point in history that has made the issue in question globally important. Basically, the idea has been to go back far enough in history to avoid the reader from being obliged to ask the famous "but why?" question. Although, on many of the most crucial issues today in global studies, you could go almost endlessly further and further back into history, finding yet another historical reason for why something takes place today. The idea when writing Visions for the Global Economy was not to go too far back so as to not make this book 600 plus pages, but rather a comfortable 200 page read. Visions for the Global Economy was written in the interest of finding a key turning point in history—whether it be a major conference, Summit, treaty, convention, or initiative; which contributes to why the global issue at hand is relevant to our global economy today. For example, a "key turning point" in the climate change debate is shown in the Conference of Parties (COP) to the UN Framework Convention on Climate Change (UNFCCC) held in 1997 in Kyoto, Japan, which created today's Kyoto Protocol.

Visions for the Global Economy combines foundational aspects, arguments, and key turning points in history to provide a holistic approach to global issues. This book's approach is helpful for students and teachers alike, especially those planning to study or teach foreign affairs, international economics, global studies, or any other related social science.

Thematically, Visions for the Global Economy addresses Economic Growth, Global Economic Governance, and Political Economy—all of which provide us with a solid base for understanding the increasingly complex world today. The global economy has changed exponentially over the last decade and a half. Today, students cannot exclusively study politics or economics. They need to study both. Students need to have a good grasp of the political economy. And if you are a student of Global Studies, you need to have a good grasp of the "global" political economy. Some of our planet's most pressing economic challenges are being held up for political reasons. Reading Chapter eight on "The Political Economy of the Eurozone", you will witness this first hand.

Additionally, today's "student of the world", whether he or she focuses his or her studies in Political Science, Economics, or International Relations—must have a good understanding of Finance. One of the most profound aspects of globalization (and definitely the least understood, especially by nonfinancial experts) is finance. When your professor, friend, or colleague tells you the world "has gone global", you could respond by saying it has also gone "financial". Basically, finance, like technology and trade, has become one of the primary drivers of globalization. A "financialization" of the world economy has taken course and probably nothing has demonstrated this more than the 2008 global crisis. It was born in the US, but quickly became global in scale. Another example is the 2011-2012 Eurozone crisis and the preoccupation it poses among financial investors and decision makers all over the globe. Multiple chapters throughout Visions for the Global Economy cover financial issues, especially aspects related to past financial crises.

Visions for the Global Economy also addresses the financial dimension of commodities. Nobody appreciates when the price of food or gas shoots up; except maybe financiers on Wall Street, or institutional investors in Chicago, London, or other major financial cities around the world. Volatile commodity prices are a dangerous issue today, and any expert of Global Studies needs to have a firm knowledge of the commodities market—how commodities are sold, who controls them, who invests in them, which countries grow and export them, who benefits when they are sold, who suffers when they become too expensive, how they are regulated—in the US and Europe, etc.

Also, you do not have to be an environmentalist to be interested in climate change. Chapter nine entitled "The World Outgrows Kyoto—A 20th Century Agreement in a 21st Century World", which addresses climate stability as a global public good, shows you that the climate crisis is just as much a crisis of politics, macroeconomics, and global leadership; as it is one of environmental proportions.

I hope Visions for the Global Economy becomes a powerful source of motivation. I hope students read these pages and begin to understand that although the issues throughout these chapters may be complex, one thing is simple; they all demonstrate, in some form or another, that there is a global leadership deficit worldwide.

I would want students to read this book and begin to feel that they are useful to global economic governance, and that they are ready to play a role in its daily events because they have a core understanding of the key global issues that extend across newspapers and computer screens daily. I would want students to acquire the ability and courage to go out and debate these issues. I would want students to feel they have the ability to propose solutions in accordance with their own visions for the global economy. I hope that students of Global Studies read Visions for the Global Economy and realize that the potential of their young bright minds, combined with their knowledge and understanding of these issues, leaves us all with a deep sense of hope that tomorrow will be a better day.

John R. Gagain Jr.

PART I
ECONOMIC GROWTH

Chile experienced a massive wheat boom in the mid nineteenth century, which then crashed late that century to early twentieth century; while also suffering other booms and busts particularly in its primary commodity of copper. Chilean copper suffered at least three major commodity boom episodes: the first associated with the Korean War in the 1950s, the second associated with the Vietnam War in the 1960s; and the third associated with the increasing financial bubble starting in 2002, that led up to the world financial crisis in 2008 (Velasco, Lecture Session 3, Pg. 11).

While all these commodity boom episodes were taking place, every commodity rich country misbehaved (both before and during such booms); ranging from the worst of examples (i.e. Mexico), to the only "well behaved" exception (i.e. Norway). Bad fiscal policy in commodity rich countries was common throughout the last five decades (Velasco, Lecture Session 3, Pg. 7). These countries were overwhelmed with a two-dimensional problem—meaning, not only were commodity rich countries posed with the challenge of significant fluctuations in the price of commodities (i.e. oil, copper, etc.), but they were also confronted with fluctuations in capital flows.

Capital flows lending to commodity rich countries are procyclical (Velasco, Lecture Session 3, Pg. 5). This meant that when "times are bad" (international) banks did not want to lend to you. Your country would end up facing a "borrowing constraint" (most likely even at a time when your country needed financing to stimulate your economy). During the boom (i.e. the "good times"), lending constraints would be lifted and you would be allowed to borrow as much as you want. Therefore, during high commodity price booms; instead of saving (as you should for a rainy day), lending and spending typically increase; and during commodity busts, borrowing constraints are posed.

Mexico is the worst of examples, where from 1973 to 1990, fiscal deficits showed a direct correlation with increasing oil prices. Mexico showed that despite significant revenues, it ran fiscal deficits (Velasco, Lecture Session 3, Pg. 7). Not to mention, during commodity boom episodes, when the revenues (i.e. the "spoils") are high, you have what is called the "voracity effect", meaning greater political activity and intervention to gain from such spoils. This creates an "endogenous borrowing cycle", with everyone "politically" wanting more of the spoils, generated by commodity prices, and the Minster of Finance taking loans to spend and suffice these interests; compounded by an exogenous commodities cycle of the volatile booms-and-busts (Velasco, Lecture Session 3, Pg. 8).

Evidence shows, however, that commodity rich countries have begun, since 2000, to reverse this trend, after having realized that commodity boom episodes are temporary, and controlling spending (especially during the boom period before the bust arrives) is increasingly important to the fiscal health of the economy (Velasco, Lecture Session 3, Pg. 14). Commodity rich nations began to establish fiscal policy rules; and as of 2000, the International Monetary Fund (IMF) estimated that eighty countries had established some sort of fiscal policy rule at the national level (Velasco, Lecture Session 3, Pg. 20).

Chile, however, has had relatively strong "budgetary institutions and positive fiscal performance" since the country's transition from the dictatorial regime of General Augusto Pinochet to democracy in 1990 (Velasco, Lecture Session 3, Pg. 22). Chile had begun to understand in the early years of its recent modern democracy, the importance of addressing commodity market volatility. Chile began the creation of the "Chile Copper Fund", which would set aside revenues specifically as a means of dealing with the fiscal challenges presented by booms-and-busts in the market; however, these efforts went no further than a joint letter of intent between the Chilean Government and the World Bank (Velasco, Lecture Session 3). It was not until 2001, at the initiative of then Chilean Minister of Finance Nicolas Eyzaguirre, that Chilean President Ricardo Lagos adopted a self-imposed fiscal rule. At the moment, this was appropriate and sufficient, considering the political environment and macroeconomic and financial situation of the country (Velasco, Lecture Session 3).

In 2006, however, President Michelle Bachelet, who succeeded President Lagos, decided it was important to be a "true progressive" by ensuring sustainable and continuous access to social services; whether the price of Chilean copper was high or not, and whether the commodity market was in the midst of a commodity boom episode or not. Therefore, with the help of then Chilean Minister of Finance Andres Velasco, President Bachelet achieved Congressional support to pass the Fiscal Responsibility Law of 2006, which legally established Chile's fiscal policy rule (Velasco, Lecture Session 3, Pg. 26).

Although Chile maintained relatively responsible fiscal policy since its transition to democracy in 1990, the country believed it lacked a "long-term fiscal policy framework", particularly considering the growing volatility of commodities and the increasing booms-and-busts. Chile understood that volatile revenues meant volatile expenditures. Chile wanted to have the ability to forecast stable and recurrent revenues in addition to commodity revenues in general (Velasco, Lecture Session 3, Pg. 22). The rule, especially due to its "flexible" and "credible" nature, the latter due to expert input; allowed Chile to be able to replicate the kind of behavior that theory depicts, in this case: responsible fiscal policy depicting deficits in bad times and surpluses in good times; hence allowing for such an ideal fiscal situation, which has not been the trend over the last fifty years.

Trade liberalization and complementary policies
High commodity prices can easily be perceived as positive for the economic growth of developing countries (especially "commodity rich" developing countries), but evidence on commodity price booms (outlined in the previous section on Chile's structural budget rule) shows otherwise—demonstrating that such an assertion is not so simple (or true for that matter).

The same goes for trade liberalization. Freeing up trade does not generate a positive cause and effect relationship nor automatic "magic bullet solution" for economic growth either. Trade liberalization, quite often, requires complementary policies. Some trade liberalizations have led to prosperity, opportunity and economic diversification in some countries; while other countries have experienced limited results (World Bank 2005, Pg. 133). This often leads to rejection of trade and globalization by the "anti-globalizers" who occupy the streets of cities that are home to World Trade Organization (WTO) Round negotiations or global meetings of the Washington DC-based international financial institutions. The World Bank shows that this controversy is provoked by trade liberalization measures because trade is merely "an opportunity, not a guarantee" and "there are many possible ways to open an economy" (World Bank 2005, Pg. 133).

Two key elements required for "successful integration" into world trade are policies that support infrastructure development and strengthening and improving national institutions (World Bank 2005, Pg. 141). These policies would help to overcome the "binding constraints" that often make trade liberalization a daunting challenge in terms of increasing exports and economic growth. These essential "complementary policies" are referred to as the "behind-the-border agenda" (World Bank 2005, Pg. 141); and often serve as the target(s) of "aid-for-trade" schemes, which aim to provide direct assistance to least developed countries and developing countries engaged in a process of trade liberalization (OECD, Pg. 3).

In the realm of infrastructure, the most pressing issue is transport. The greatest challenge to the competiveness of exports in many developing countries is the high cost of transport, particularly from rural developing country communities, that are home to farmers and impoverished citizens looking to harness the opportunities of trade liberalization (World Bank 2005, Pgs. 142143). For example, in Malawi high transport costs have weakened competitiveness and profitability of firms and farmers (…) and although this country is an efficient producer of sugar, "domestic transport costs account for fifteen percent (or more) of local consumer prices" while "regional and international transport costs account for fifty percent of the mill production costs" (World Bank 2005, Pg. 143).

Rodrik, Subramanian, and Trebbi find that "quality of institutions 'trumps' everything else"; and although, their findings show this, they also illustrate that trade has a "positive effect on institutional quality"—much to the effect of a mutually reinforcing and beneficial relationship in the interest of trade liberalization as a force for economic growth (Rodrik, et. al. Pg. 3). In other words, trade liberalization needs institutions and institutions need trade.

No example demonstrates this more than Jamaica and Mauritius, both of which "shared the same per capita GDP in 1984"; but thereafter, "between 1984 and 2000, real per capita GDP grew at approximately 4.8 percent a year in Mauritius, compare with only 0.7 percent in Jamaica" (World Bank 2005, Pgs. 142). Surprisingly, this "disparate growth performance could not be attributed to differences in trade", because 1985 to 2000, show that real annual growth of exports in both nations was more-or-less on par (i.e. Mauritius 3.9 percent and Jamaica 3.6 percent). In 2000, trade in Jamaica "accounted for a larger share of GDP" than in Mauritius (World Bank 2005, Pgs. 142).

The difference in growth performance between these two countries is supported by two key factors: "institutional quality and macroeconomic stability"; which exemplify "Mauritius's superior institutions (democracy and strong participatory institutions), and ethnic diversity, that provides integral links to the rest of the world, as well as the importance of participatory political institutions that contribute to maintaining stability, rule of law, and mediating conflict", which helps Mauritius to do a better job in "government effectiveness, political stability, rule of law, control of corruption (…) with the rule of law being a particular problem in Jamaica, amid crime and violence costing Jamaica at least 4 percent of GDP" (World Bank 2005, Pgs. 142).

In addition to institutions, macroeconomic stability is an important component of trade reform, particularly in Latin America, which has been known for quite some time as the world's "most economically and financially volatile region" (Rojas-Suarez, Pg. 1). In this respect, low inflation and stable and competitive exchange rates stand to play a pivotal role, as Latin American countries seek to liberalize trade and make the appropriate reforms for doing so, while enhancing growth. The key to success in this exercise in policymaking, however, lies in the ability to be able to assume trade reforms as "part of a broader package of reforms" (…) while also finding the "trade reforms that complement others reforms leading to an identification problem" and a need to "sequence" the series of reforms determined (OECD, Pg. 32). Consequently, the Center for Global Development (CGD) set out a framework for the analysis of the reforms undertaken in the interest of furthering economic growth throughout Latin America.

The Center for Global Development Framework
There has been a plethora of studies conducted that examine the "theory of growth acceleration" and the "diagnostics of growth" in developing countries (Rojas-Suarez, Pg. 5); however, Hausmann, Rodrik, and Velasco have taught us that countries "need to identify the single most important binding constraint" if they are to implement policies that are "growth promoting" (Rojas-Suarez, Pg. 18.). Every country is different and every country has its own set of policies that would need to fit in terms of enhancing economic growth, because policies that "work wonders in some places may have weak, unintended, or negative effects in others" (Hausmann, Pg. 1). The same goes for regions. Not every region shares the same set of socioeconomic, political, or cultural attributes; hence the rationale behind why the CGD utilized distinct Latin American characteristics as a basis for designing their Analytical Framework for Economic Growth (Rojas-Suarez, Pg. 6).

A task force of Latin America's top experts, all of whom developed the "region-specific" CGD framework, based it upon "three characteristics that distinguish Latin America from other regions. Latin America is the most democratic and most financially open region (more so that East Asia, which is more open to trade). Latin America also has the greatest levels of economic and social inequality (Rojas-Suarez, Pg. x). As Latin America ranks as the most financially open region of the world; global capital markets, consequently play a "significant role in assessing the appropriateness of policies and reforms" as they "reward the implementation of policies and reforms that strengthen the functioning of markets" or "penalize those that constrain it" by moving capital accordingly (Rojas-Suarez, Pg. 21). Therefore, the first three (of five) foundations for growth of Latin America (contained in the CGD Analytical Framework) coincide with an "institutional approach" supportive of the "adequate functioning of markets" (Rojas-Suarez, Pg. 21).

The first three foundations address: secure property rights, sufficiently equal opportunities for broad segments of society, and sufficient economic and political competition (Rojas-Suarez, Pg. 21); and without these three "market-based growth" is deemed "not possible" (Rojas-Suarez, Pg. 22). The last two (foundations four and five) are deemed as essential to the "sustainability" of market-based growth. These last two include: macroeconomic stability and the broad sharing of the benefits of growth among the population (Rojas-Suarez, Pg. 22).

Secure "property rights" will help citizens, particularly investors (both domestic and foreign), to be able to "expect to benefit from their investments" while reducing the chances that their investments are "unexpectedly expropriated by the State or the political powerful" (Rojas-Suarez, Pg. 54). The second foundation for growth referring to "sufficiently equal opportunities for broad segments of society" will contribute to a "leveling of the playing field" in market-based interactions; which means, "lowering barriers of entry to investors (or business people) that possess no political connections (Rojas-Suarez, Pg. 55). "Sufficient economic and political competition", although it sounds similar to foundations one and two, will help to ensure that the State does not "funnel" a disproportionate quantity of resources to "a relatively few favored individuals or companies" (Rojas-Suarez, Pg. 55).

The fourth foundation regarding "macroeconomic stability" is inherently important due to Latin America's frequent economic and financially plagued history dating back to the 1980s. As a result of these historical characteristics, any measures that aim to sustain growth in Latin America must consistently maintain macroeconomic stability in order to reduce the probability that investors (and capital) would "flee at the first sign of trouble", which would create and deepen whatever financial difficulties that exist at the country level—while potentially leading to an increasingly exacerbated crisis (Rojas-Suarez, Pg. 55). Finally, the fifth foundation regarding the need for "broad sharing of the benefits of growth among the population" is important if governments are to create and maintain reforms that are not rejected by a considerably large portion of the population in Latin America. A small portion of the population corresponds to "investors" that relate to the preceding foundations of growth outlined in this Analytic Framework. The majority of citizens in Latin America work as "employees or in small-scale independent activities, or are outside the labor force" working in the informal sector, studying in school or university, living as a dependents, or collecting a pension (Rojas-Suarez, Pg. 55). This foundation means that growth must be democratic. Growth must respond to the needs (of the majority) of citizens, hence the reason why many governments in Latin America have made "redistributive policies" (Rojas-Suarez, Pg. 56).

All of these five foundations for economic growth in Latin America are important in their own right, however, there are certain elements that may present obstacles (or prevent reforms), even if each one of the five foundations is taken into consideration during the reform process at the national level. One distinct challenge has been the "lack of needed sequencing" (Rojas-Suarez, Pg. 59). As a largely open region—in economic and financial terms, it is important to sequence reforms in Latin America. For example, the experience with "trade reform" in the region provides cases that demonstrate this "common design problem" where "the capital account was liberalized simultaneously with the current account", which "eroded potential gains from trade" due to a "real appreciation of the exchange rate" (Rojas-Suarez, Pg. 59). This also led to an increased amount of "banking crises" in the region, as seen in the last two decades of the twentieth century, due to the fact that financial markets were "liberalized" before an "appropriate supervisory framework" was put in place (Rojas-Suarez, Pg. 59).

A good country example for effective "sequencing" of reforms is India. India experienced macroeconomic stability and "impressive export and growth performance in the 1990s" because it depreciated its real exchange rate first, before starting to liberalize trade (World Bank 2005, Pg. 141). This "sequencing of reforms" in India increased export incentives and "cushioned the impact of lower import barriers on domestic industry". India prudently sequenced trade liberalization first, before opening its capital account; and, as a result, India's real exchange rate has remained moreorless at the same level since 1992, which has "facilitated trade reforms" (World Bank 2005, Pg. 141).

Poverty and Jobs in Latin America
It is commonly known that economic growth is a catalyst for achieving gains in development and poverty reduction. For example, the World Bank indicated "for every one percent of economic growth, poverty declines by an average of 1.25 percent in Latin America" (World Bank 2006, Pg. 57). On the other hand, it is less known whether poverty has an impact on economic growth. The same findings of the World Bank, however, demonstrated just recently that not only does growth help reduce poverty, but poverty reduction can help promote growth— hence leading to the creation of virtuous circle in favor

of development gains. The World Bank specifically highlight that poverty itself can have a "negative and strongly significant impact on growth" where on average "a 10 percent increase in poverty reduces annual growth by 1 percentage point" (World Bank, 2006, Pg. 116).

Acknowledging the mutually supportive role that growth and reduced poverty levels play, Professor Andres Velasco puts forth an innovative approach for dealing with poverty and jobs in Latin America. Perhaps his motivation for doing so could be highlighted by the moderate (or less than moderate) levels of growth in Latin America, most of which are particularly insufficient for reducing poverty, especially at levels adequate enough for achieving the UN's Millennium Development Goals. As the most unequal region of the world, and one plagued by poverty and limited gains in poverty reduction, (particularly compared to poverty reduction levels of Asian countries, which enjoy growth levels that exceed Latin America), Professor Velasco envisioned a need to rethink the approach to addressing poverty and jobs.

To be able to understand and appreciate Professor Velasco's innovative approach, one first needs to understand how poverty is measured and evaluated. Traditionally, poverty is measured in absolute terms, according to income levels (establishing a poverty line between the poor and the non-poor) or what is more commonly considered, especially in Latin America, as access to a basket of the most basic goods required for survival. The latter is referred to as Unsatisfied Basic Needs, or as it is more commonly referred to in Spanish—NBI (Necesidades Básicas Insatisfechas). The way in which poverty is measured thwarts policy outcomes and concrete action towards reducing poverty and extreme poverty. Not to mention, this also lessens the possibilities of focusing on the root causes of poverty. The traditional approaches to measuring poverty treat poverty as a one-dimensional problem with one solution. More importantly, it lessens the chances of displaying the true social problem that exists in Latin America, which is inequality. It is important to note that inequality normally refers to "income inequality", most likely due to the limitations of current poverty measurements.

When addressing both poverty and inequality, the question of access to employment is indispensable. Current political democracy tends to focus on end problems; and more particularly, on the "end need" of citizens. If a citizen is hungry, the citizen's end need is food. If a citizen is poor, the citizen's end need is money, or better yet, the source of money, which is a job. Therefore, the end problem in this case (i.e. lack of a job) is unemployment. Professor Velasco's approach innovatively addresses these problems—poverty, inequality, and unemployment; by presenting a new approach.

This new approach includes harnessing the "better (best) data" that exists at the national level, which then permits the policymaker to utilize data based upon the root cause of the problem rather than the end cause of the problem (or problems). Professor Velasco uses a "household" approach to poverty and jobs, rather than the traditional and one-dimensional "income-based" approach (Velasco, Lecture Session 8, Pg. 4). Also, his approach is not based upon the "individual citizen" as is normally utilized when measuring poverty or inequality, as in the case of arriving at a Gini Coefficient when determining inequality. Professor Velasco's approach on the other hand, focuses on "per capita household income (PCHY)" (rather than Gini Coefficient) as a means to measuring poverty and inequality, and more importantly, the causes and dimensions behind them. This approach, not only allows a multidimensional focus, but also allows such a multidimensional focus to highlight important factors such as access to opportunities (i.e. decent employment), social and culture problems, and human capacity issues (i.e. twenty-first century job skills).

Professor Velasco's argument for utilizing this new approach to addressing poverty and employment is based upon the fact that many countries have taken a "very partial" approach to addressing "inequality"; and evidence shows that the "difference between what determines a rich household and a poor household, is simply not an issue of the head of the first household making X versus the head of the next household making Y, but also a matter of how many people are in each household, as well as how many people in each household 'are working', and bringing home an income" (Velasco, Lecture Session 8, Pg. 2). The argument behind Professor Velasco's approach is based upon the fact that "differences in access to employment" are equally important in causing "inequality" as differences in access to a "well-paid job" (Velasco, Lecture Session 8, Pg. 2).

Professor Velasco's approach utilizes Chile as fertile ground for analyzing poverty and inequality, as well as a concrete example for where anomalies could exist when using the old approach to measuring and evaluating poverty (i.e. individual income) versus the new approach (i.e. household employment). For example, although Chile is a strong performer in most areas including democratization, institutions, growth, and poverty reduction; Chile is largely an unequal society. Measuring with a Gini Coefficient, Chile's inequality is unprecedented in the region; however, utilizing Professor Velasco's approach, Chile's status as an unequal society is found to be even worse than previously known. Chile has "mediocre employment performance" and does poorly in what Professor Velasco considers to be the "race to employment" (Velasco, Lecture Session 8, Pg. 4).

Professor Velasco's approach takes this equation L = E + U + D (Labor Force = Employed + Unemployed + Discouraged) and develops "employment ratios" (i.e. not "unemployment ratios") based upon E over L (rather than the typical discussion, which is normally about U over L), due to the fact that in many countries the real problem is not exclusively one of "unemployment", but more so a problem of "low participation" (Velasco, Lecture Session 8, Pg. 11). Professor Velasco's approach uniquely captures both problems (i.e. unemployment and low participation). His particular use of this equation creates an ability to analyze, not only the difference of "income distribution" between E, U, and D; but more important an analysis "amongst those that work" (i.e. E), which Professor Velasco shows by dividing the country into "deciles"—and comparing the poorest decile to the richest decile; hence the poorest ten percent of Chile to the richest ten percent of Chile (Velasco, Lecture Session 8, Pg. 6).

Professor Velasco's findings on his analysis demonstrate two important points: first, the distribution of employment opportunities varies widely across deciles in Chile; and second, when comparing the distribution of employment opportunities in other countries with Chile, it shows that employment rates vary widely across countries in Latin America (Velasco, Lecture Session 8, Pg. 11). Particularly, the differences in access to employment for the richest decile versus the poorest decile in Chile—shows that access to employment for the richest ten percent hovers close to eighty percent, while employment for the poorest ten percent of the Chilean population hangs at twenty-five percent; highlighting, not only the inequality from decile to decile in Chile, but also its relation to the poorest and richest deciles of other Latin American countries (Velasco, Lecture Session 8, Pg. 11).

The findings indicate that most unemployment in Chile resides in the poorest decile. The findings also indicate that Chilean inequality is driven by the tremendous disparity between the deciles on the two opposite ends—the poorest versus the richest; and Professor Velasco's calculations show, that if he were to remove the poorest ten percent of the population and the richest ten percent, and were to compare inequality between the second decile and the ninth decile—meaning the "second poorest" and "second richest" deciles respectively; inequality in Chile would instead be on par with Sweden—a country that is known for its large levels of equality (Velasco, Lecture Session 8, Pg. 14).

Variations in the findings as a result of assumptions made by Professor Velasco, show that there is a "higher education gap" in Chile, meaning that the richest decile are all university educated citizens that earn proportionately much greater than the poorest decile. When analyzing the "income distribution among those who work" in Chile, the findings show that the 10/10 ratio between the poorest decile and the richest decile is 17.7 percent (Velasco, Lecture Session 8, Pg. 13). When taking into consideration the "household income distribution" meaning the amount of the members of the household that work versus those that do not work—hence the households in the poorest decile (which are traditionally larger) vis-à-vis the richest decile you end up with a 10/10 ratio of 46.2 percent (Velasco, Lecture Session 8, Pg. 14). Note the increase in inequality disparity from 17.7 percent to 46.2 percent. Also, this more accurate calculation that takes into consideration the size of the household, shows us that hardly anyone in the poorest decile works and almost everyone in the richest decile works.

When taking into consideration the "per capita household income distribution", meaning dividing for the average number of members of a household (i.e. average household size is 3.6 in Chile) you end up with a 10/10 ratio of 78.5 percent. This last finding shows that the poorest households earn an average per capita income of US $31, which is equal to the World Bank standard for living in extreme poverty (i.e. living on less than US $1.25 per day PPP). This last finding worsened because another source of disparity was added—this disparity was the addition of the "size" of the household; and the last was the addition of the "unemployed" in the household (Velasco, Lecture Session 8, Pg. 15). Once again, these findings in their entirety show that inequality has little to do with "wage disparity" and a lot to do with "differences in access to employment" and "differences in access of household size" (Velasco, Lecture Session 8, Pg. 15). These findings also show that the "number of people who work" per household makes a big difference as well as the "number of members" of the household—and both variables are very unevenly distributed across income deciles in Chile (Velasco, Lecture Session 8, Pg. 16).

Most importantly, this analysis of Chile, when adapted for certain variations displays incredible potential results. For example, if all households with a per capita income less than the national average in Chile are taken under the assumption that, in each of household, the number of people (ages 1864) who work is equal to the national average, this would lead to a 120 percent increase in household income; and that would reduce the 10/10 ratio from 78.5 percent to 36.8 percent. A second example shows, that if all households were taken under the assumption that, in each decile, the employment ratio for women is the same as that of men, the results show that the household income for the poorest decile would surge by 35 percent, reducing the 10/10 ratio from 78.5 percent to 63.4 percent. These reductions in inequality of the 10/10 ratio show, when compared to Gini Coefficients, a reduction in the Gini Coefficient of Chile of four points—from 0.58 to 0.54, which is revolutionary in the realm of economic and social development and combating inequality.

This new approach to analyzing poverty, inequality and employment is revolutionary and innovative. If it receives proper followup and attention, it could promote incredible results for policymaking at the national level. This approach shows that "there is no one factor that keeps the impoverished from having access to regular employment".

It does show, however, that the most challenging problems in Chile reside in the poorest decile. Those who are affected by inequality and poverty in the poorest decile are women, youth, the physically challenged, and rural inhabitants. More specifically in the poorest decile(s) households have more children under the age of four, more women and youth (that are the majority of the unemployed), and more Chilean citizens with the "least schooling" (Velasco, Lecture Session 8, Pg. 23-31).

Multidimensional poverty indices
Similarly to the way in which Professor Velasco developed a new "household" approach, based upon analyzing "access to employment", as a new and innovative form of evaluating poverty and inequality, "multidimensional poverty indices" do the same. Poverty deals with much more than merely having enough money in your pocket (to resolve your needs) and the needs of your family. Poverty is a question of having the basic capacities to be able to provide for your human development as well as that of your family.

In order to reduce poverty and make progress in the longterm, public services, business action (i.e. corporate social responsibility measures, etc.), and the efforts of civil society organizations will need to be channeled and targeted towards meeting the basic concrete needs of the impoverished in the areas of education, health, gender equality; access to housing, potable water, and sanitation, and employment, etc. if Latin America is to overcome poverty and inequality at the speed necessary for achieving the UN's Millennium Development Goals by their deadline of 2015. These actions will require mechanisms that measure concrete achievements, while simultaneously leading to more improved and better targeted policy interventions. These different measurement mechanisms reach beyond "income poverty" and address the "multidimensionality" of poverty [i.e. Human Opportunity Index (HOI – World Bank), Human Development Index (HDI – UNDP), and the Multidimensional Poverty Index (Alkire & Foster– Oxford University)] (Trebatt, Lecture Session 9, Pg. 23).

The different dimensions of multidimensional poverty indices help to ensure that the income index is joined by a health related index (i.e. life expectancy) and an education index, which together afford poverty reduction strategies with a more holistic and sustainable approach, while taking into consideration longterm economic and social development needs (Trebatt, Lecture Session 9, Pg. 23). This is the only viable approach that ensures the economic dimension (i.e. economic growth) is supported by the social and environmental dimensions and vice-versa— therefore making economic growth a positive force for all the citizens of Latin America.

BIBLIOGRAPHY

Bulmer-Thomas, Victor, John Coatsworth, and Roberto Cortes-Conde. The Cambridge Economic History of Latin America: Volume 2, The Long Twentieth Century. Cambridge: Cambridge University Press, 2006.

Dominguez, Jorge I. "Explaining Latin America's Lagging Development in the Second Half of the Twentieth Century, Growth Strategies, Inequality, and Economic Crises." Falling Behind: Explaining the Development Gap Between Latin America and the United States. Francis Fukuyama. New York: Oxford University Press, 2011. Location 1508, Kindle E-Edition.

Hallaert, JeanJacques. "Increasing the Impact of Trade Expansion on Growth: Lessons from Trade Reforms for the Design of Aid for Trade", OECD Trade Policy Working Papers, No. 100, OECD Publishing (2010): pgs. 1-42.

Hausmann, Ricardo, Dani Rodrik, and Andres Velasco. "Growth Diagnostics." Harvard University John F. Kennedy School of Government (March 2005): Pgs. 1-35.

Humphreys, Macartan, Jeffrey D. Sachs, and Joseph E. Stiglitz. Escaping the Resource Curse (Initiative for Policy Dialogue). New York: Columbia University Press, 2007.

Rodrik, Dani. "Goodbye Washington Consensus, Hello Washington Confusion?" Journal of Economic Literature, Vol. XLIV (December 2006): pgs. 973–987.

Rodrik, Dani, Arvind Subramanian, and Francesco Trebbi. "Institutions Rule: The Primacy of Institutions Over Geography and Integration in Economic Development." Harvard University (October 2002): Pgs. 145.

Rojas-Suarez, Liliana. Growing Pains in Latin America, An Economic Growth Framework as Applied to Brazil, Colombia, Costa Rica, Mexico, and Peru. Washington DC: Center for Global Development, 2009.

Sachs, Jeffrey D., and Andrew M. Warner. "The Curse of Natural Resources." European Economic Review 45 (2001): Pgs. 827838.

Trebatt, Thomas. Lecture Session 2: Latin America in the Twentieth Century: How and Why the Region Fell Behind. (REGN 6423, Problems of Economic Growth in Latin America, SIPA, Columbia University). 19 September 2011.

Trebatt, Thomas. Lecture Session 4: Toward a Framework for Economic Growth in Latin America. (REGN 6423, Problems of Economic Growth in Latin America, SIPA, Columbia University). 03 October 2011.

Trebatt, Thomas. Lecture Session 5: The Role of the External Sector I Trade and Growth in Latin America. (REGN 6423, Problems of Economic Growth in Latin America, SIPA, Columbia University. 10 October 2011.

Trebatt, Thomas. Lecture Session 9: Persistent Problems II: Poverty, Inequality, and Economic Growth. (REGN 6423, Problems of Economic Growth in Latin America, SIPA, Columbia University. 31 October 2011.

Velasco, Andres. Lecture Session 3: Natural Resource Wealth and Fiscal Policy: The Case of Chile. (REGN 6423, Problems of

Economic Growth in Latin America, SIPA, Columbia University). 26 September 2011.

Velasco, Andres. Lecture Session 8: Persistent Problems I: Jobs and Inequality in Latin America. (REGN 6423, Problems of Economic Growth in Latin America, SIPA, Columbia University). 24 October 2011.

World Bank. Economic Growth in the 1990s: Learning from a Decade of Reform. Washington DC: The World Bank, 2005.

World Bank. Poverty Reduction and Growth: Virtuous and Vicious Circles. Washington DC: The World Bank, 2006.

Zettelmeyer, Jeromin. "Growth and Reforms in Latin America: A Survey of Facts and Arguments." IMF Working Paper. (July 2006): pgs. 139.

CHAPTER 2
THE CHALLENGES OF PEACE AND ECONOMIC GROWTH IN COLOMBIA

Growth is a hot item today. Market based democracies around the world are embracing economic growth as a primary development goal of their democratic regimes more than ever before—not only in "words", which may be for reasons related to political democracy (hence the fact that economic growth generates employment opportunities); but also in "deeds", as we have seen concrete policy reforms being taken with the aim of achieving improved economic growth levels nationwide.

For this reason, the Center for Global Development, the renowned Washington DC-based think tank dedicated to reducing global poverty and inequality through rigorous research and active engagement with the policy community, organized a Task Force to consider the impact of policy reforms on growth (Rojas-Suarez, pg. x). The Task Force's work led to the creation of a framework whose aim was to analyze regionspecific growth. The framework was applied to Brazil, Colombia, Costa Rica, Mexico and Peru and published in Growing Pains in Latin America (Rojas-Suarez, pg. x).

The Task Force's framework included the establishment of five "foundations" of growth, for which it considered inherently important to achieving marketbased growth, particularly in Latin America. The five foundations include secure property rights, sufficiently equal opportunities, sufficient economic and political competition, macroeconomic stability, and broad sharing among the population of the benefits from growth (Rojas-Suarez, pg. 22).

According to Growing Pains in Latin America, the "five foundations cannot be prioritized; all must be built simultaneously" (Rojas-Suarez, pg. 22). This aspect of the framework seems to have served as a principal challenge for the aforementioned Latin American countries as they strived to achieve growth in recent decades, while also adapting and focusing on the needs and challenges of their national policy environments.

Colombia is a good case in point. A comprehensive reform effort began in 1990, comprising a "set of market-driven reforms aimed at enhancing competition and the role of the private sector, as well as, institutional reforms aimed at strengthening macroeconomic stability, promoting equality of opportunities in the political and judicial arenas, and sharing more broadly the benefits of growth across regions and individuals" (Rojas-Suarez, pg. 111).

The problem, however, was that "reforms aimed at strengthening some foundations for growth actually weakened others." The underscoring example behind this problem included the fact that the "benefits of broadened opportunities achieved through fiscal decentralization, increased social expenditure, and expanded access to the judicial system" were accompanied by "fiscal deterioration and macroeconomic vulnerability" (Rojas-Suarez, pg. 111).

In 1988, then Colombian President Virgilio Barco proposed initiating a process of drastically reforming the country's 100-year-old Constitution, which had undergone limited reforms since its inception in 1886. President Barco's intention was to reinvigorate a new political consensus among the nation's sectors and actors. There was a need to enhance governance and facilitate the containment of the drug cartels as well as the peace process with the guerilla movements (Rojas-Suarez, pg. 114).

In 1991, Colombia's new Constitution created its thirty-two provinces, known as departments, along with a Capital District. This process of decentralization included "a central government transfer of a large portion of tax revenue to these departments and municipalities "in order to finance a meaningful expansion of expenditure in health and education (Rojas-Suarez, pg. 114). Additionally, the 1991 Constitution empowered citizens to appear before a court to demand adherence to their fundamental rights, known as "acción de tutela". It also gave unprecedented power and independence to the Constitutional Court and the Central Bank, introduced fully funded private pension funds, further liberalized trade and finance, and made for a more flexible labor market (Rojas-Suarez, pg. 114 & 120).

The reforms successfully laid the foundations for future market-based economic growth. In the interest of financial liberalization, "Law 9 of 1991 removed all entry restrictions and established national treatment for foreign direct investment...dismantling capital controls that had been in place for over twenty years" (Rojas-Suarez, pg. 120). With respects to labor market flexibility "establishing a labor union was made simpler and the restrictions forbidding labor union members from participating in politics were repealed" (Rojas-Suarez, pg. 121). In terms of decentralization, the 1991 Constitution increased the amount of resources transferred from "wealthier to poorer regions" in order to ensure broad access to health and education (Rojas-Suarez, pg. 121).

Holistically, the Constitutional Reforms established the legal concept of an "estado social de derecho", which is important to ensuring, not only access to "first generation" civil liberties; but also "second generation" rights, including access to certain services, which require the State's action in support of the economic and social rights of its citizens (Rojas-Suarez, pg. 124).

The reform process, on the other hand, was not completely free from challenges or inconsistencies. Some policies proved fiscally unsustainable, particularly the expansion of social expenditures through the decentralization process. Other policies moved workers (back) to the informal sector, fostered political party fragmentation, and converted the Constitutional Court into a veto power when it came to economic policy (Rojas-Suarez, pg. 124).

The newly introduced "tutela" mechanism, although it gave greater judicial recourse to citizens concerning their economic and social rights; it also created economic, fiscal, and institutional inefficiencies. According to El Tiempo newspaper, "between 1999 and April 2007, 1.6 million tutelas were filed, one-third of them in reference to health care...where the judiciary upheld 87 percent of the total" (Rojas-Suarez, pg. 125). This compromised the State's fiscal and macroeconomic stability.

Contributing further to jeopardizing Colombia's fiscal stability, the Constitutional Court decided that "a 1993 decision granted to compensate 'some' retired teachers whose pensions were not adjusted for inflation", be extended to "all" pensioners; which cost approximately 12.5 percent of GDP (Rojas-Suarez, pg. 126).

It seems a majority of the Constitutional Court's judgments were considered critical to the macroeconomic and fiscal health of the nation. The most controversial decisions, however, according to the CGD Task Force, were those dealing with the financial sector (Rojas-Suarez, pg. 126). Consistently on the grounds of "equality", the Constitutional Court's decisions posed grave challenges to the banking sector. For example, after the government introduced a "financial transactions tax (FTT) and exempted it from interbank operations, the Court overturned this provision on the grounds that it violated the principle of inequality", which "dried up" the interbank market and foreign exchange operations for a period of time (Rojas-Suarez, pg. 126). Also, while the government "forced banks to accept properties returned by 'low-income' mortgage holders in exchange for the complete write-off of their mortgage; the Constitutional Court, once again, in accordance with the principle of equality, extended it to all debtors, not just low-income (Rojas-Suarez, pg. 126).

The reforms throughout the 1990s left Colombia with a high-level of fiscal pressure as well. The transfers from the national to the subnational level were some of the highest in the region; while additionally by 1999, Colombia "had the second-highest non-wage labor costs in the region; which, according to the World Bank (2005) showed that the rise in non-wage costs had constrained the demand for labor while increasing supply" (Rojas-Suarez, pg. 130). These non-wage costs entailed many government entitlement programs, which rose in contributions from 7 percent to 12 percent in 1993, and to 12.5 percent in 2007 (Rojas-Suarez, pg. 130). These ever increasing levels of public expenditures required Colombia to engage in multiple tax reforms, which had a negative effect on competition and efficiency.

According to the CGD Task Force, two factors play a role in the "fiscal deterioration" that overwhelmed Colombia: one, "the overestimation of the fiscal benefits of the 1993 pension reform"; and, two, the "rising expenditures" particularly due to the 1991 Constitutional mandates (Rojas-Suarez, pg. 136). Worse than merely a process of fiscal deterioration, the reforms of the 1990s in Colombia did not make clear as to how the expenditures would be assigned in terms of levels of government. The 1991 Constitution called for Congress "to pass a territorial organization law distributing assignments", however this did not take place (Rojas-Suarez, pg. 139).

It could be said that decentralization coupled with the strengthening of the provision of services in health and education could be the primary cause having a negative effect on competition and efficiency; however, although challenges remain in both sectors, whether it be the excessive cost of universal health coverage or teacher wages, there has been success in this area. The 1993 reform devoted to health care enabled coverage to rise from 47 percent of the Colombian population in 1996 to 74 percent in 2005; prompting the UN's World Health Organization to rank Colombia first among its 191 member countries with regard to fairness of contributions and financial risk protection (Rojas-Suarez, pg. 139). In the area of education, Colombia now spends more per capita on public education than any other large country in the region (Rojas-Suarez, pg. 141). School enrollment has increased, particularly among the lowest quintiles, with the bulk of improvement and attainment taking place in the rural areas and in favor of girls (Rojas-Suarez, pg. 142).

The CGD Task Force shows that "although several reforms undertaken in Colombia since 1990 strengthened some of the foundations for growth, other reforms had unintended consequences"; with the "most salient" example being "fiscal decentralization", which the CGD Task Force deemed having had "adverse effects on macroeconomic stability" (Rojas-Suarez, pg. 144). They also believe that the related judicial reforms have left a "high fiscal price tag" particularly due to the role the tutela plays in the Constitutional Courts decisions related to economic and social rights of citizens coming before it (Rojas-Suarez, pg. 144).

The CGD Task Force recommends that certain aspects of the acción de tutela be reviewed in order to curtail the system's ability to tamper with economic policy matters (Rojas-Suarez, pg. 145). They also recommend, in accordance with an avenue put forth by "former associate justice Uprimmy", that "Colombia's level of development should inform Constitutional Court rulings, with some rights being achieved progressively over time, rather than immediately" (Rojas-Suarez, pg. 145). Uprimmy proposed a "consensual definition" by all powers of what should "constitute an adequate health care plan, so that judges will no longer uphold tutelas demanding services beyond what the plan includes (Rojas-Suarez, pg. 145). The CGD Task Force also recommends that judges on the Constitutional Court, who serve for eight years, and then enter the political arena; should otherwise be required to take a "cool off period" of at least five years before being allowed to run for elected office (Rojas-Suarez, pg. 145). This would help to eliminate any potential connection between decisions made on the bench affording citizens awards in favor of their second generation Constitutional Rights and a potential future political democratic electoral process in Colombia (Rojas-Suarez, pg. 145).

The CGD Task Force also recommends a series of proposals for overcoming the adverse effects on macroeconomic stability posed by fiscal decentralization, all of which lean towards an overall need to clarify the distribution of responsibilities among levels of government (Rojas-Suarez, pg. 148).

According the CGD Task Force, the 1990 reforms in Colombia "should have had a positive impact on the foundations for growth", going even further to consider that the "initial drive for reform", meaning those begun in 1988 by President Barco "failed to deliver on many of its expected promises…in particular Colombia's longheld adherence to macroeconomic stability" (Rojas-Suarez, pg. 149).

Let me offer a different perspective.
First, it is important to mention the moment in history when Colombia began these reforms in 1990. At that moment, nationally, Colombia was probably at its peak in terms of violence, drug trafficking, narco-terror, guerilla warfare, kidnapping, and death.

The 1995 homicide rate was 69.7 for every 100,000 inhabitants (UNODC 2011). Externally, that same year brought the fall of the Cold War, communism, and the Berlin Wall; hence the fall of the same political ideology that contributed to so deeply dividing Colombia, making it a politically bipolar society, throughout the 20th century. Therefore, 1990 was a promising moment for Colombia, one where it stood at a crossroads, which required Colombians to rethink the future of their country as well as the source of violence that plagued their nation for a century. Colombia needed to make reforms, not only for the sake of economic growth, but more so for spreading the benefits to populations that have traditionally not benefited from economic growth.

There is no one size fits all for development. Every country and community is different; and a country like Colombia, with Colombia's levels of violence and divisive history, has no other choice, but to make more equitable access to the benefits of economic growth as a main goal, and a driving force for its policy reforms—otherwise with continued extreme levels of violence; any economic growth in Colombia stands jeopardized in the long-term.

Second, these reforms addressed an "accumulated social debt" and divided society that could be traced backed to the 1930s, and what was known as La Violencia—a period of organized violence lasting from the mid-1940s to mid-1950s. Therefore, the inequality and lack of social justice that plagued Colombian society needed to be addressed, particularly as an inherent cause of the decades of violence taking place throughout the country. Therefore, these reforms started in the 1990s, began an economic and social paradigm shift; which did not take immediate effect, but began a process of second-generation development enshrined in the Colombian Constitution.

It is true that these reforms did put macroeconomic stability, competition, and perhaps market efficiency at risk during the reform process; however, the intentions of those governmental actors and desired results were most likely not anticipated immediately. It is quite probable, that considering the levels of violence, division, poverty, and inequality that existed, the Colombian authorities knew they were at a life changing moment in the life of their nation that would require years, if not decades, to take hold. A little macroeconomic instability would not hurt.

The CGD Task Force ended by noting that the "reform process was eventually reinvigorated and many of the design problems of the initial reform drive had been addressed...and the process, coupled with a benign external environment and a much improved security situation, has of late produced enormous benefits in terms of economic growth and a renewed decline in poverty" (Rojas-Suarez, pg. 150). Something must have worked. Development is a process. That same homicide rate is today cut in half. What use to be a rate of 69.7 for every 100,000 inhabitants now hovers at 33.4 (UNODC 2011).

BIBLIOGRAPHY

Rojas-Suarez, Liliana. Growing Pains in Latin America, An Economic Growth Framework as Applied to Brazil, Colombia, Costa Rica, Mexico, and Peru. Washington DC: Center for Global Development, 2009.

Pécaut, Daniel. Las FARC: Una Guerrilla Sin Fin o Sin Fines?. Bogotá: Grupo Editorial Norma, 2008.

Center for Global Development (CGD). 2011. www.cgdev.org/section/about/mission

El papel del ex presidente en la gestación de la Constituyente de 1991, Virgilio Barco, el precursor olvidado. Humberto de la Calle. 28 June 2011. El Espectador. www.elespectador.com/impreso/politica/articulo280613virgiliobarcoelprecursorolvidado

Global Study on Homicide. 2011. UN Office of Drug Control and Crime Prevention. http://www.unodc.org/documents/dataandanalysis/statistics/Homicide/Globa_study_on_homicide_2011_web.pdf

PART II
GLOBAL ECONOMIC GOVERNANCE

CHAPTER 3
THE GLOBALIZATION OF CITIZEN-TO-CITIZEN BASED GROWTH

As of recently, a global shockwave of protests have arisen; whether it be the Arab Spring, riots in London, housing price protests in Israel, student marches in Chile, the destruction of "fat cats'" expensive cars in Germany, increasing discontent in China, or the "Occupy Wall Street" movement in New York and other States across the USA; somewhere someone is voicing rejection for the havoc that inequality continues to wreak on society worldwide (Roubini, Pg. 1).

Inequality is traditionally measured by the Gini coefficient. Named after a prominent twentieth century Italian economist, the Corrado Gini coefficient is a number ranging from 0 to 100, which determines the value of countrywide distributions—zero if all citizens have the same income, and 100 if the entire income of a community is appropriated by one person only (Milanovic, Location 194).

As the Gini coefficient has served as a benchmark for measuring inequality, particularly by providing a country-to-country range; we have since witnessed inequality existing not only country-to-country or "among" countries, but also "within" countries; which has led to a "dual divergence" amongst developing countries where some developing countries are left behind; while others surge ahead, essentially "catching up" in the race of economic development and global competitiveness. This shows us that inequality is not necessarily any longer a question of country-to-country growth levels or industrialized versus developing countries; but more so, an issue of growth as it relates to the quality of "citizen-to-citizen" (Ocampo, Pg. 8). Hence, this is part of the reason why researchers are also using the population-weighted (or unweighted) GDP growth, instead of measuring GDP-weighted GDP growth to determine development progress globally.

Such weighted (and/or unweighted) measurement has become increasingly important due to the uneven progress taking place as a result of heavily populated countries like China and India having had excelling growth rates, while other considerably less populated developing countries have not. As Milanovic displays, weighted versus unweighted measurements of inequality are important primarily because of China and India; because you get two different outcomes if you take these two countries out of the global measurement equation (Milanovic, Location 199). Global poverty and inequality would seem to be decreasing when actually they is not.

As a result, developing countries have begun to question the determinants of growth. They question whether China, India, or other emerging economies will be able to sustain their respective growth levels. They ask if Chinese and Indian growth levels will imply growth for them as well. They want to know if globalization is (or has been) beneficial for their country; and if so, how to (continue) convert(ing) it into a positive force for their peoples.

Growth successes (and collapses), however, have tended "to cluster" in specific time periods over the past half century, with "global economic developments" having played an important role in this outcome (Ocampo, Pg. 11). A large part of our challenge has been our ability to fully understand the "determinants of economic growth", especially as new complexities in this realm are being rediscovered (Ocampo, Pg. 26).

Economists alike are fostering a consensus, which states that the determinants of growth are often "country-specific"; and, that "policies needed to create such conditions (for economic growth) are not reducible to 'simple formulas'" or a onesizefits all approach (Ocampo, Pg. 26). They believe these are (were) grounds for rejecting the 'Washington Consensus' of the 1990s, which embraced the notion that "economic prosperity is a matter of getting a particular set of the national policies 'correct'" (Ocampo, Pg. 26).

Rodrik highlighted that "nobody really believes in the Washington Consensus anymore" (Rodrik, Pg. 974). The "question now is not whether the Washington Consensus is dead or alive; it is what will replace it"; because "there are no confident assertions here of what works and what doesn't—and no blueprints for policymakers to adopt. The emphasis is on the need for humility, for policy diversity, for selective and modest reforms, and for experimentation" (Rodrik, Pg. 974).

Although this approach seems sensible, "initial conditions are not merely 'country-specific'" in that "they also interact with conditions specific to regional location and the 'dynamics of the global economy'" (Ocampo, Pg. 26). Ocampo states that "initial conditions are difficult to manipulate and countries with "poorer endowments" have greater difficulties in positioning themselves to benefit from world economic growth" as a result of "world market imperfections" that "compound trends towards divergence" (Ocampo, Pg. 27).

Examples include:

- One, countries with "poor endowments" have "greater disadvantages" in international trade, finance, and the global reserve system;
- Two, capital flows tend to concentrate among richer countries;
- Three, more than 80 percent of foreign direct investment to developing countries moves to a small number of mostly middle-income countries;

- Four, unskilled migrant workers face many obstacles abroad;
- Five, technological progress is highly concentrated and diffusion is slow due to trade barriers and intellectual property rights;
- Six, no clear debt mechanisms have been established in international financial markets leaving an advantage for international lenders rather that developing countries;
- Seven, voting power and leadership in key international institutions including the OECD, IMF, and World Bank are limited to industrialized countries;
- Eight, asymmetries in the policy space for conducting macroeconomic policy exist due to developing countries not having the option to issue liabilities in their own currency, which leaves vulnerability to exogenous shocks such as fluctuations in the interest rate denominated in another currency;
- Nine, developing countries find it difficult to participate in World Trade Organization negotiations, which require abundant resources for studies and participation, and;
- Ten, development aid has become politicized and driven by economic objectives of the donor countries, rather than targeted towards the developmentrelated needs of developing countries (Ocampo, Pg. 27-30).

The pursuit for growth, assumed by developing countries alike, needs to address domestic "binding constraints" (Rodrik, Pg. 974); although, it should not discard the global asymmetries presented by globalization currently. Any approach to sustaining economic growth and overcoming inequality, requires both domestic and global cooperation—only then will all developing nations begin to achieve a growth that each and every citizen desires inherently enshrined in the potential benefits economic globalization presents for all societies.

BIBLIOGRAPHY

Milanovic, Branko. Worlds Apart: Measuring International and Global Inequality. Princeton: Princeton University Press, 2005.

Ocampo, José Antonio, and Rob Vos. Uneven Economic Development. New York: United Nations, 2008.

Rodrik, Dani. "Goodbye Washington Consensus, Hello Washington Confusion". Journal of Economic Literature Vol. XLIV (December 2006): 973987.

Roubini, Nouriel. "The Instability of Inequality." Project Syndicate. After The Storm (2011).

CHAPTER 4

G7, G8, G20 AND THE G193: THE PROLIFERATION OF THE "GS" AS A MEANS FOR DEALING WITH THE CHALLENGES FACING THE WORLD ECONOMY

Throughout the latter half of the 20th century, most structural developments in international politics took course as a result of the pervasive fear of the spread of communism. The birth of the G7, deeply inspired by the same motivating force, comprised additional reasons, which included the tattered reputation of the United States internationally in the 1970s, as well as, the ideas of US Secretary of State Henry Kissinger (Bradford, Pg. 19).

Kirton lists the aforementioned challenges confronting the US, starting with President Richard Nixon's unilaterally imposed "10 percent import tax on America's closest friends" and the elimination of "currency convertibility", which had made the "US dollar as good as gold", not to mention the "halt of trade after the Tokyo Round in 1973", the "1973 oil shock", a nuclear empowered India, the spread of "Euro-Communism", the threat of Soviet default on "loans from Western Banks", the "bankruptcy New York faced and President Gerald Ford's refusal to bail the city out", US defeat in the Vietnam War; and the "Watergate scandal" (Bradford, Pg. 19).

Taking into consideration these challenges, as well as America's need to "stave off its crisisbred decline" and Kissinger's belief that an "embattled democratic West" would benefit from "a cohesive Atlantic community" and "modern democratic global concert"; the Group was formed with the United States, France, Germany, Italy, Japan, and the United Kingdom as its initial core participants. Canada was added shortly thereafter at the second Summit held in Dorado, Puerto Rico, in 1976, to make for the complete G7 (Bradford, Pg. 20).

The communiqué of its first Summit held in Rambouillet, France, highlighted the political motivations behind the creation of the G7 by stating "We are each responsible for the government of an open, democratic society, dedicated to individual liberty and social advancement" (Bradford, Pg. 20). It highlighted (related) key issues covered of its agenda including: international finance, macroeconomics, employment, trade, development, a "commodity-empowered South", a "new international economic order (NIEO)", and an "orderly and fruitful increase in economic relations with 'socialist countries' as an important element of progress in détente" (Bradford, Pg. 20).

The G7 achieved success, which included "stopping a second holocaust in Europe", advancing its political agenda regarding the issue of Kosovo, and waging a "successful campaign against apartheid in South Africa"; however, its greatest triumph was "peacefully winning the Cold War and post-Cold War peace" (Bradford, Pg. 21-22). This later led to the inclusion of Russia in 1997 into an enlarged G7— hence converting it into a G8. Coincidentally, Soviet leader Mikhail Gorbachev's "surrender letter" was addressed to the "G7 leaders" rather than the United States (Bradford, Pg. 21).

The same year Russia was added to the Group, the East Asian financial crisis sent shockwaves throughout the global economy. In the wake of the crisis, an "informal forum for discussion among officials of G7 countries and a select group of 'systemically significant' developing countries" was taking place (Bradford Pg. 36). In 1998, the G7 engaged Australia, Hong Kong, Singapore, the Netherlands, and "a number of relevant international financial institutions to establish the Financial Stability Forum (FSF)" whose goal was to "enhance the exchange of information, cooperation, and financial supervision and surveillance to promote international financial stability, while improving the functioning of markets and reducing systemic risk" (Martinez-Diaz, Pg. 21).

In 1999, finance ministers and central bank governors of G7 countries announced their intention to "broaden the dialogue on key economic and financial policy issues among systemically significant economies and promote cooperation to achieve stable and sustainable world economic growth that benefits all" (Kirton, Pg. 5). This announcement brought to fruition the G20. Overtime however, the influence of the G20 (as a group of Finance Ministers) waned, until the 2008 financial crisis (Bradford Pg. 37).

It was not until the peak of the 2008 financial crisis that the G20 (at the level of Heads of State and Government) was born. President George W. Bush wanted to demonstrate that his administration was committed to "preventing a global economic breakdown". In late 2008, he recognized that the "changed world called for a 'broader group', so he asked to speak to officials from the G20, then chaired by Brazil". After being persuaded by French President Nicolas Sarkozy and others, President Bush convened "the first G20 Summit in Washington DC in November 2008" (Zoellick, Pg. 2). Since, the G20 has played the role of global "responder" and "preventer" of economic crisis and "defender" of globalization (Bradford Pg. 14). At its Pittsburgh Summit in 2009, the G20 designated itself "the premier forum for our international economic cooperation" (G20 Pittsburgh Summit, 2009).

In 2010, the G20 took a symbolic firststep by holding its Summit in a nonG8 member country. The historic Seoul Summit helped the G20 to transition from a "crisis management committee" to a "global economic steering committee" (Bradford Pg. 62). The Summit "made substantive contributions to the G20 by presenting financial safety nets, development, and reform of the Bretton Woods Institutions as new agenda items" (Bradford Pgs. 5758). Additionally, the Summit brought light to "Korea's successful development experience" and "efforts to become a global Korea"

(Bradford Pg. 57). Most importantly, the Summit emphasized, "economic development in developing countries is closely linked with economic recovery in the developed countries" (Bradford Pg. 57). This notion is particularly important for the 2011 G20 Summit in Cannes, France.

The primary challenge threatening the world economy is the danger of a double dip recession, particularly in the US and Europe. Already, unemployment is burgeoning; and there is a dire need to get the economy growing. An advisor to President Sarkozy stated, "France would like to adopt a 'true action plan for world growth' at the Cannes Summit (Hilimoniuk, Pg. 3). The Cannes Summit, however, may suffer from issue fatigue due to an overextended agenda, which includes: noncooperative jurisdictions and tax havens, the Multilateral Convention on Mutual Administrative Assistance in Tax Matters, the international monetary system, financial regulation, commodity price volatility, employment, the social dimension of globalization, corruption, and development—not to mention, the crisis happening in the European Union regarding Greece and Italy consumes the global economic agenda.

A foreseen challenge stems from what President Sarkozy and the Cannes Summit will decide regarding the future of the G7/G8. Not moving forward on this issue would be "a step backward for President Sarkozy, as he was ready to enlarge, (indeed to take the leadership in enlarging) the G8 to the G13/G14" (Bradford, Pg. 54). The issue puts the cohesiveness of the G20 in jeopardy; particularly when the G20 would like to strengthen its role, and (if anything) extend its inclusive spirit to emerging economies. After all, the more the G20 desires to consolidate its role as the premier forum for international economic cooperation, it is going to find itself having to rely upon the leadership and direction of economically emerging developing countries from the G193.

BIBLIOGRAPHY

Bradford, Colin, and Wonhyuk Lim. Global Leadership in Transition: Making the G20 More Effective and Responsive. Washington DC: Brookings Institution Press, 2011.

G20 Pittsburgh Summit. John Kirton. 2009. Munk School of Global Affairs at the University of Toronto. 2011. <www.g8.utoronto.ca/g20/summits/2009 pittsburgh.html>

G20 Plans and Preparations – Cannes Summit. Ryan Hilimoniuk. 2011. Munk School of Global Affairs at the University of Toronto. 2011. <www.g20.utoronto.ca/g20plans>

History of the G20. John Kirton. 2007. Munk School of Global Affairs at the University of Toronto. 2011. <www.g20.utoronto.ca/docs/g20history.pdf>

Martinez-Diaz, Leonardo, and Ngaire Woods. Networks of Influence?: Developing Countries in a Networked Global Order. Oxford: Oxford University Press, 2009.

Zoellick, Robert B. "Five myths about the G20". Washington Post. 28 October 2011.

CHAPTER 5

BRIDGING THE ECONOMIC AND SOCIAL DIMENSIONS OF GLOBAL GOVERNANCE

Since more than half a century ago, the United Nations has been discussing and making efforts to reform its organization's international cooperation mechanism in the economic and social field. Martens claims that recommendations oriented towards economic and social reform from expert commissions and government initiatives have "amassed enough to fill libraries" (Martens, Pg. 3). He states that "for the past 50 years there have been continued attempts to either reform the UN's Economic and Social Council (ECOSOC) or to create an entirely new global decisionmaking body for economic and social matters" (Martens, Pg. 3).

Many of these reforms efforts have contemplated the establishment of completely new institutions (or measures) including the creation of a "World Economic Council", a Council for Sustainable Development, a Global Governance Group, an "L20" or "Leaders 20 Group", and an Economic Security Council (Martens, Pg. 4). It was this last option, the Economic Security Council (ESC), as Marten claims, "that has appeared in many reform initiatives since the mid-1980s" (Martens, Pg. 4). Dervis explains that proposals regarding an ESC have been addressed by the "1995 Commission on Global Governance" in their well-known report "Our Global Neighborhood" as well as by the "2003 Rasmussen Report"; with endorsements from the "Panel on Financing for Development led by former Mexican President Ernesto Zedillo" and Economics Professor Joseph Stiglitz (Dervis, Pg. 96).

The ESC seems to have been a formidable approach to reforming the economic and social dimensions of global governance; particularly due to its "decentralized character", which allows currently functioning UN agencies as well as the Bretton Woods Institutions (BWIs) to continue to function according to their specialized roles. Dervis explains that the ESC, as proposed, would "not interfere" in the workings of these institutions (Dervis, Pg. 100).

The key question, however, is why, after more than fifty years of attempted economic and social reforms, and close to thirty years of attempts to establish an ESC, have these reform efforts remained unsuccessful?

Careful consideration and reflection warrants two possible reasons. First, the impetus for reforming the economic and social dimensions was thwarted, overbearing, and intrusive. Never should the motivation for such reforms been the inaccuracies and imperfections of the G7; especially with it having been the most powerful group of national economies of the 20th century. Second, the ESC's conceptual approach lent itself to being perceived as potentially invasive and authoritative, particularly to those UN specialized agencies and BWIs it had hoped to regroup under an "ESC umbrella" (Dervis, Pg. 98).

The outcome of the Commission on Global Governance should never have pitted the ESC against the G7; particularly by highlighting the G7's imperfections, (i.e. "under representative nature"), as a means for justifying the importance of creating an ESC—especially considering the historical background, origin, and rationale behind the creation of the G7, which included a volatile Cold War geopolitical setting, combined with "America's need to "stave off its crisisbred decline" and belief that an "embattled democratic West" would benefit from "a cohesive Atlantic community" (Bradford, Pg. 20).

The Commission's report stated the G7: is the nearest the world comes to having an apex body concerned with the global economy (…) but it is neither representative of the world's population as a whole nor very effective. The G7 represents only 12 percent of the world's population (...) it can no longer even claim to represent the world's major economies. The development issues that concern most of humanity have low priority on its agenda. Looking decades ahead, it will become more and more anachronistic (...) (Global Neighborhood, Pg. 154).

Aside from targeting the G7's imperfections, the proposed ESC's institutional profile was remarkably similar to that of the G7, hence resembling an attempt to supersede this Group. The Commission's report stated the ESC's primary task would be to "look at the main trends in the world economy (...) and also have a role in responding to acute crisis" while having a membership that would first and foremost include "the world's largest economies (Global Neighborhood, Pg. 157-159).

The proposed ESC duty of "appoint(ing) all heads of institutions" (UN specialized agencies and BWIs) was considered "crucial" to the ESC's institutional responsibilities (Dervis, Pg. 99). This task, however, has been a role reserved (and assigned) to the UN Member States currently occupying the Executive Boards and Councils of these UN agencies and BWIs and/or the UN SecretaryGeneral himself. Additionally, the ESC would acquire an additional function as "external evaluator" of performance and policy (Dervis, Pg. 100101). Consequently, combining these two proposed tasks of ESC, that being the functions of "hiring and evaluating", could only lead the ESC to be perceived as the entity in charge of "firing" as well— only by default when the ESC decides to hire the next head of agency or BWI.

The ESC may have had a chance at survival if it was not pit against the G7 or compared to two increasingly complicated UN agencies—one, the UN Security Council, an organ that stubbornly prefers to disserve the 21st century geopolitical reality by remaining adequate only for a 20th century post-World War II era; and second, the ECOSOC, an organ of which the Commission calls for its demise, while simultaneously using it as a point of reference for the creation of the ESC (Global Neighborhood, Pg. 263).

The language behind the creation of the ESC also shunned any support from current influential governments. Aside from the proposed power of hiring, firing, and evaluating; the ESC would now include "intellectuals" rather than "bureaucrats", as if bureaucrats had little (if any) intellectual capacity (Global Neighborhood, Pg. 160). The language running throughout the conceptual proposal for an ESC was too harsh and drastic; and not amenable to a complex body that requires democratic support for institutional change.

In order for the ESC to work, it would first need to receive the approval of the international establishment; and today that ranges from the UN Security Council's "P5" (permanent five), the G20, to the G77, among others. Although its been on the stove's back burner for quite sometime, the ESC would have a chance at survival if two things were to happen: one, the G7/G20 (and the UN agencies and BWIs that their governments serve) were not threatened by an ESC; and two, the same agencies and BWIs alternate "chairmanship" of the ESC. Until then, the remaining predominant venues for economic (and social) cooperation and discussion will continue to be reserved to forums including the G20, G8, and the World Economic Forum in Davos.

BIBLIOGRAPHY

Bradford, Colin, and Wonhyuk Lim.Global Leadership in Transition: Making the G20 More Effective and Responsive. Washington DC: Brookings Institution Press, 2011.

Dervis, Kemal, and Ceren Özer. A Better Globalization: Legitimacy, Governance, and Reform. Washington DC: Center for Global Development, 2005.

Martens, Jens (2006), "The Never-ending Story of ECOSOC Reform: L27 as emerging alternative to G8?", World Economy and Development In Brief, Issue 5 (2006) (www.wdev.eu).

The Commission on Global Governance. Our Global Neighborhood: The Report of the Commission on Global Governance. New York: Oxford University Press, USA, 1995.

CHAPTER 6

THE PARADOX OF APPLYING NATIONAL REGULATIONS TO A GLOBAL MARKET: A REVIEW OF COMMODITY FUTURES

Since the mid nineteenth century, farmers, producers, and other market participants have been able to engage in the trade of commodity futures contracts; whose purpose has been to allow a farmer, for example, the opportunity to lock in a price (in the future) for his or her crop before harvest time, potentially when faced with unexpected market volatility posed by changes in weather, supply, demand, or political uncertainty, etc. (Dunn, Pg. 8). Futures trading has allowed farmers to bring their goods to a central market exchange; the first of which was established in 1848 in Chicago, Illinois; more formally known as the Chicago Board of Trade (CBOT), which still exists today (Das, Pg. 25).

These commodity futures contracts, also known as "derivatives", could be thought of as "bets on the price of something", which provide a buyer or seller with "insurance" and the opportunity to manage "risk" (McDonald, Pg. 2). These bets gave rise to the concept of "financial speculation". Consequently, economists "differentiated gambling and speculation on the grounds that gambling involves the deliberate creation of new risks for the sake of diversion, while speculation involves the assumption of the inevitable risks of the capitalist process" (Chancellor, Pg. xii). The practice of financial speculation led to the conceived notion of a market actor known as a "financial speculator". Economist Joseph Schumpeter highlighted that "the difference between a speculator and an investor can be defined by the presence or absence of the intention to 'trade'" (Chancellor, Pg. xi).

The nineteenth and early twentieth centuries were not free from financial experimentation, shenanigans, and instability. Speculators pervaded the market, some with the intention to trade physical goods (as in the case of the bona fide physical hedgers mentioned above), while others did not and only looked to take advantage of trends in the market to wager their way towards profit margins. The commodity futures market expanded beyond the traditional exchange, the typical contracts, and the customary agricultural products; to where today, the market includes hedging and speculating on commodities such as "crude oil, heating oil, gasoline, gold, and silver", as well as others (Gensler, Pg. 01). Speculation became particularly rampant in the 1920s, and then it led to the Crash of 1929 (Johnson, Location 613). Almost a decade later, on the heels of President Franklin D. Roosevelt's New Deal, the principal legislation governing commodity futures markets was formed—the Commodity Exchange Act (CEA) of 1936, which "originally applied only to derivatives on domestic agricultural products" (Financial Crisis Inquiry Commission, Location 1576).

This CEA had to be amended in 1974; to reflect that "futures (and options) contracts on virtually all commodities, including financial instruments, be traded on a regulated exchange" (Financial Crisis Inquiry Commission, Location 1576). It was this legislative revision that created the independent federal agency known today as the Commodity Futures Trading Commission (CFTC), whose task is to regulate and supervise the futures market ("History of the CFTC"). Despite this regulated environment, however, "an over-the-counter (OTC) market began to develop and grow rapidly in the 1980s", its creation motivated by the concern of the "large financial institutions" who were "acting as OTC derivatives dealers" most of whom "worried that the CEA's requirement that trading occur on a regulated exchange might be applied to the products they were buying and selling" (Financial Crisis Inquiry Commission, Location 1581).

Around the same time, particularly in 1981, a big change occurred in the market, with the introduction of a "new derivatives product" referred to as a "swap" (Gensler, Pg. 2). Swaps, developed by the banks and trade dealers themselves, were coined as agreements between two parties in the market; more or less, like a side bet, outside the realm of the actual market itself. Shortly thereafter, for some reason most likely coinciding with the laissez faire ideology of the 1980s, which served as an impetus for the deregulation of markets (supported and championed by US President Ronald Reagan and US Federal Reserve Chairman Alan Greenspan), the CFTC in 1989, "exempted swaps from the CEA" and stated that "to avoid regulation, swaps must be negotiated by the parties as to their material terms, based upon individualized credit determinations, and documented by the parties in an agreement or series of agreements that is not fully standardized" (Greenberger, Pg. 4).

Subsequently, the swaps marketplace grew and ended up playing a pivotal role in the destruction of the global economy that led to the financial crisis of 2008. Burgeoning and unstable capital flows flooded this market, leading it to balloon, from less than US $1 trillion in total (notional) amounts in the 1980s, to a notional value of approximately $300 trillion in the United States" in 2011 (Gensler, Pg. 2). Hence, this led to an economy where "for every dollar in the US economy, there was US $20 of swaps" (Gensler, Pg. 2). This has been coined the "financialization" of commodity trading—more formally defined as the "increasing role of financial motives, financial markets, and financial actors in the operation of commodity markets"; which has taken course because "investors have been engaging in commodities trading for the purpose of portfolio diversification ever since it became evident that commodity futures contracts exhibited the same average returns as investments in equities" (UNCTAD, Pg. 13). A major problem, however, is that commodities have been increasingly viewed as an "asset class", as if they were a financial investment such as a "stock". Commodities are not financial assets (i.e. stocks, bonds, mutual funds, index funds, exchange-traded funds) and therefore, should not be traded as such (Dicker, Location 938).

In 1998, the CFTC circulated a "concept release on OTC derivatives", which found that these financial products were "almost certainly subject to the mandatory exchange trading requirements (and therefore were trading in violation of law)" (Greenberger, Pg. 6). The CFTC concept release was accompanied by a public inquiry, which was motivated by the fact that "unregulated swaps had caused so many financial calamities", whereby a 1997 US Government Accountability Office (GAO) Study reportedly identified "360 substantial end-user losses" while the CFTC cited a report that listed "22 examples of significant losses in financial derivatives transactions" (Greenberger, Pg. 6). Despite these losses, the work of the CFTC was "strongly opposed", particularly by fellow US Government Agencies that served alongside the CFTC on the President's Working Group on Financial Markets. At the request of these agencies—the US Department of Treasury, the US Federal Reserve Bank, and the US Securities and Exchange Commission (SEC); US Congress eventually "enacted a six-month moratorium to the CFTC concept release" (Greenberger, Pg. 7).

Later that same year, Long-Term Capital Management (LTCM), the US's largest and most successful hedge fund, "nearly collapsed from the loss of over a period of weeks of US $4.6 billion (approximately 90% of its capital) on losses from OTC derivative positions (Greenberger, Pg. 7). For fear of LTCM creating a shockwave of losses throughout the global economy, LTCM received a bailout of US $3.6 billion; similar to those the large financial institutions received with US tax payer-funded assistance in 2008 (i.e. AIG, Bank of America, Citigroup, JP Morgan Chase, Fannie & Freddie Mac, etc.) (Greenberger, Pg. 7). As a result, the President's Working Group on Financial Markets recommended "expanded authority" to require "OTC derivative counterparties to provide credit risk information, recording-keeping, reporting data, trading strategies, and risk models"; while

Federal Reserve Chairman Greenspan "declined to endorse this set of recommendations, although he deferred to those regulators with supervisory authority (Greenberger, Pg. 8).

Additionally, "twelve of the world's largest banks formed the Counterparty Risk Management Policy Group (CRMPG) to conduct a 'self-study of practices' that led to the LTCM crisis and to recommended self-regulatory practices that would prevent such an episode from reoccurring" (Greenberger, Pg. 8). The CRMPG, nevertheless, vehemently "opposed new regulation" highlighting that "it would be a mistake to attempt to codify risk management practices in that fashion" and further recommended to US Congress that "financial OTC derivatives should be totally deregulated, because regulation could discourage the growth of swaps markets and drive them elsewhere" (Greenberger, Pg. 9). Consequently, US Congress passed on 21 December 2000, and US President William J. Clinton signed into law the Commodity Futures Modernization Act (CFMA) of 2000, which "removed OTC derivatives transactions, including energy futures transactions, from all requirements of exchange trading and clearing under the CEA so long as the counterparties to the swap were 'eligible contract participants'" (Greenberger, Pg. 9).

As a result of the CFMA, the commodity futures market changed forever; or at least until 2008, when it exploded—or what is more formally known as the bursting of the "commodities bubble". New actors increased their entrance to the market, known as "index speculators", most of whom represented "institutional investors" or institutions such as investment banks, hedge funds, money market funds, endowments, pension funds, etc.—all of which were looking towards commodities as an asset class with the interest of investing in a "broad basket of commodities" rather than having any interest in any "individual commodity" (Masters and White 2008, Pg.

29). These investors are referred to as "massive passives", due to their massive size and their "fairly price-insensitive, passive trading strategy" where they inject capital into the market and ride their investment in search of long-awaited returns (Chilton, Pg. 2).

Normal supply and demand has always had an effect on the prices of commodities; however, for the first time, there has been a massive "new source of artificial financial demand" that had also contributed greatly to higher prices where "institutional investors poured hundreds of billions of dollars into the commodities futures markets as part of a portfolio allocation decision" (Masters and White 2008, Pg. 12). An analysis of financial capital flows into commodity markets throughout a five year span between 2003 and 2008, showed that "commodity index investment rose by a factor of 25 times from US $13 billion to US $317 billion" (Masters and White 2008, Pg. 14). Commodity prices tripled, and one of the clearest indications, which pointed toward index speculators as a driver of higher prices was that "every single one of the 25 commodities, which make up the S&P GSCI (Standard & Poors, Goldman Sachs Commodity) and DJ-AIG (Dow Jones-American International Group) indices had risen substantially" during the same five year period (Masters and White 2008, Pg. 14). There are signs that show that capital flows into speculative investment positions have continued, and have even surpassed 2008 levels—the peak of the world economic and financial crisis. As of 2011, speculative positions increased to their highest levels ever with the "number of futures equivalent contracts held by 'massive passives' increasing by 64 percent in energy contracts and by 20 percent (or more) in metals and agricultural contracts between June 2008 and January 2011" (Chilton, Pg. 3).

Therefore, the same supply and demand, which has always had an effect on the prices of commodities, had been deceived by "uneconomic consequences" driven by this "new source of artificial financial demand". No better verification exists than the financial bubble that led the price of oil to dramatically rise to US $147 in July 2008. First, in 2008, the US, the world's leading consumer of oil, was already in the midst of an economic recession, which started in December 2007 (Masters and White 2009, Pg. 01). Second, data from the US Energy Information Administration (EIA) World Oil Balance 2004-2008 showed that "world oil production increased in the first and second quarters of 2008 (US Energy Information Administration). Hence, demand was low, supply was high; and crude oil prices defied the recession and the laws of economic supply and demand by climbing an astonishing 60 percent from US $90 per barrel of oil in January 2008 to its peak of US $147 per barrel in July 2008, while dropping during a six month period by an unprecedented 75 percent to US $33 in December 2008 (Masters and White 2009, Pg. 03).

The same speculative investment in financial derivatives that led the prices of important commodities like oil, food, and minerals to surge, drop, and eventually bust (while surging again in 20102011) was not only the cause of the 2008 financial crisis, but it played a significant role (Gensler, Pg. 2). These financial derivatives "added leverage to the financial system with more risk being backed by less capital (...), contributing to a system where large financial institutions were (...) too interconnected to fail (...) while concentrating and heightening risk throughout the financial system and to the public (Gensler, Pg. 1). As a result, US Congress approved, and US President Barack Obama signed into effect, the Dodd-Frank Wall Street Reform and Consumer Protection Act (DFA) of 2010 to, among other things, bring the unregulated OTC derivatives markets under comprehensive regulation (Gensler, Pg. 2). Title VII of the DFA "transforms the regulation of OTC derivatives by requiring that swaps be subject to clearing and exchange trading, capital and margin requirements, and increased record-keeping and reporting" (Greenberger, Pg. 17).

The DFA is predicated upon what economists have agreed for decades: "markets work best when they are transparent, open, and competitive" and "transparency in the markets reduces costs" (Gensler, Pg. 2). The DFA:

> "promotes transparency by moving swaps transactions to exchanges or swap-execution facilities (SEF)" hence allowing "buyers and sellers to meet in an open marketplace where prices are made publicly available, creating a better climate for businesses to grow (...) and ensure that derivatives dealers do not have an edge over everyone else"; "reduces risk to the economy by requiring that standardized swaps go through a clearinghouse", which establishes that "clearinghouses act as 'middlemen' between two parties to a swap transaction after the trade is arranged" while requiring "derivatives dealers to post collateral so that if one party fails, its failure does not harm its counterparties and reverberate throughout the financial system"; gives the CFTC "more authority to effectively prosecute wrongdoers who recklessly manipulate the markets (...) by rewarding whistleblowers for their help in catching fraud, manipulation, or other misconduct in the financial markets"; and requires "large traders to give the CFTC data about their swaps activities and establish swap data repositories, which will gather information on all swaps transactions" (Gensler, Pg. 01).

The DFA also requires the CFTC to establish "limits on the size of futures and options positions and swap positions held by 'any person, including any group or class of traders' to achieve four goals: one, to diminish, eliminate, or prevent excessive speculation (...); two, to deter and prevent market manipulation, squeezes, and corners; three, to ensure sufficient market liquidity for bona fide hedgers, and; four, to ensure that the price discovery function of the underlying market is not disrupted (Dodd and Frank, Section 737(a)(3)(B)). Accomplishing these goals, however, has become the most controversial portion of the DFA; hence the reason why debate provoked the CFTC to finalize the rules instituting position limits on futures and swaps contracts on 18 October 2011, rather than complying with the earlier deadlines established by US Congress of 17 January 2011, for "exempt commodities" including energy commodities; and 17 April 2011, for agricultural commodities (Federal Register, Pg. 4777).

Although the CFTC passed rules for position limits on 18 October 2011, (after more than two years of deliberations and debate; which included multiple public hearings in summer 2009, January 2010, March 2010, January 2011, among other related meetings; as well as after having received more than 15,100 public comments in response to the CFTC's January 2011 public hearings, and more than 8,200 public comments in response to the CFTC's January 2010 session on energy markets), there still remains a significant difference in philosophy and agreement regarding position limits at the CFTC, particularly amongst its five Commissioners—hence the reason why these rules merely passed by a result of 3 to 2 (i.e. four Commissioners and one Chairman) (Gensler, Pg. 2).

CFTC Commissioner Michael Dunn, who served as the third vote needed to pass the position limits rule stated that "Congress has tasked the CFTC with preventing excessive speculation by imposing position limits and (...) the law is clear, and I will follow the law", however, he opined that "position limits are the 'sideshow' that has unnecessarily diverted human and fiscal resources away from actions to prevent another financial crisis" (Dunn, Pg. 02). Commissioner Dunn believes that there was no proof "or any reliable economic analysis to support the contention that excessive speculation is affecting the markets" calling the proposed position limits rule "at best, a cure for a disease that does not exist, or a placebo for one that does" (Dunn, Pg. 2). Commissioner Dunn's arguments coincide with those of the futures industry, particularly the US-based trade association "Futures Industry Association (FIA)" on position limits ("Futures Industry Association"). Commissioner Dunn retired from the CFTC in 2011, and was replaced by the new CFTC Commissioner Mark P. Wetjen.

The difference in opinion between one half of the CFTC's Commissioners and the other seems to be grounded in a difference in opinion regarding the actual purpose or modus operandi of the CFTC as a regulatory entity. Commissioner Jill E. Sommers, for example, stated in her remarks regarding position limits that the CFTC's mission is to "protect market users and the public from fraud, manipulation, abusive practices and system risk" (Sommers, Pg. 2). However, what happens when those committing the fraud, the manipulation, and the abusive practices in the market are actually the same "market users" Commission Sommers refers to? As financier George Soros stated, these "markets never reflect the underlying reality accurately, they always distort it (reality) (…) and the distortions find expression in market prices (…) and affect the fundamentals that market prices are supposed to reflect" (Soros, Location 92). Soros believes that the "financial crisis (of 2008) was not caused by some exogenous factor—like the formation of dissolution of an oil cartel—but by the financial system itself" (Soros, Location 2636). It seems that some of the CFTC's Commissioners protect the market users and some protect the public.

Commissioner Scott D. O'Malia [who agreed with Commissioner Sommers in that this vote (on the position limits rule) was the most important vote of their careers] defended the aforementioned market users by citing the US Office of Management and Budget (OMB) and stating that "each rule will have an annual effect on the economy of more than US $100 million" while forcing "commercial hedgers to invest multiple millions of dollars in developing compliance systems to justify and account for their legitimate hedging strategies" (O'Malia, Pg. 1). He stated, "if the commercial entities (...) feel like we are waging war on them, I don't blame them" (O'Malia, Pg. 2). Agreeing with Commissioner Dunn, Commissioner O'Malia questioned whether the CFTC "always knows best" and stated that the final (position limits) rules fail to articulate a convincing rationale for eliminating the current CFTC regime of "principles-based regulation" (and replacing it instead with a "prescriptive 'government knows best' regime") (O'Malia, Pg. 2). Commissioner O'Malia expressed that the current (regulatory) regime "has served the Commission (CFTC) well both prior and during the 2008 financial crisis" (O'Malia, Pg. 2).

All three Commissioners Dunn, Sommers, and O'Malia—have preached the usual argument that increased regulatory measures (i.e. positions limits) could actually make it more difficult for farmers, producers, manufactures, and others who use these futures markets (Dunn, Pg. 2). Similar critics of position limits believe that speculative positions bring "needed liquidity to the market (Pearlstein, Pg. 3). Another critic, FIA President John Damgard, publicly stated last September 2011, that the FIA welcomed the International Monetary Fund's (IMF) World Economic Outlook report, which "highlighted the important role that financial speculators have played in providing liquidity to commodity markets" ("Futures Industry Association"). The flip side of the argument, however, is that these critics of position limits "ignore the obvious dangers of having too much liquidity" in the market (Pearlstein, Pg. 3).

Better Markets, the Washington DC-based think tank dedicated to promoting the public interest in commodity markets, and specializing in the DFA rulemaking process and related global financial regulation, believes that the aforementioned "commodity index funds" (mentioned by Masters and White above)—the majority of whom are the reason behind why position limits are important—are actually "liquidity takers" rather than "liquidity providers", contrary to their critics (Kelleher, Pg. 2). Better Markets believes that index funds actually deprive "bona fide hedgers" from having sufficient market liquidity for two main reasons: first, index funds have become such a large part of the market that they often outsize bona fide hedgers— hence they have the ability to place "substantial liquidity demands on the marketplace over bounded time periods", and if they provide liquidity it is "only incidental rather than systematic" because (and this is where the second reason comes in); second, index funds' "buying and selling" is "completely unrelated to current liquidity demands" (…) due to the "view index fund managers may have on the current or future levels (or direction) of specific commodity prices" because index funds buy contracts for reasons including new investment flows, sufficient price moves, or the need to "roll" an expiring futures contract into a further out month (Kelleher, Pg. 55). In these markets, the way it is supposed to work is "liquidity providers are available when liquidity takers want to transact"; however, because of the enormous "capital inflows (or outflows), index funds—and their need to roll their positions—make it "more likely that commodity index funds will actually demand liquidity from the market" (Kelleher, Pg. 54).

Further demonstrating the severity in the level of disagreement, CFTC Commissioners Dunn and Sommers believed that the passing of the Congressionally mandated rules on position limits, undermined the very function and purpose of the CFTC as a regulating entity. Commissioner Sommers stated, "nowhere in our (CFTC's) mission is there the responsibility or mandate to control prices" (Sommers, Pg. 2). Commissioner Dunn agreed and stated, "the role of the futures market is price discovery, not price setting" (Dunn, Pg. 2). However, without position limits, "commodity index funds" stand to continue to "disrupt the commodities futures and physical markets in ways that distort price discovery (Kelleher, Pg. 2). Because index funds are "liquidity takers" they possess "large collective market positional impact", hence disrupting price discovery and diverting needed liquidity for bona fide hedgers (Kelleher, Pg. 56). This renders the market practically dysfunctional, particularly considering its original and historically intended purpose, because "today many speculators anticipate the widely publicized trading pattern of the index funds—trade based upon the institutional investor driven supply of (and demand for) futures contracts themselves, rather than the fundamentals underlying a given commodity" (Kelleher, Pg. 56).

The lack of consensus on position limits (and combating excessive speculation in commodities futures markets) extends beyond the US to the global level. Most global financial industry groups applaud Commissioner O'Malia's ubiquitous sixteen-page statement of dissent on position limits for futures and swaps ("Futures Industry Association"). The UK Financial Services Authority (FSA)'s view coincides with it as well. Commissioner O'Malia's dissent challenges whether the position limits and "limit formulas will effectively prevent or deter excessive speculation" (O'Malia, Pg. 4). FSA Chairman, Lord Adair Turner "does not believe that position limits will have a meaningful impact on controlling commodity prices", and he co-authored a study that found that "the rise in oil prices from 2003 to 2010 could largely be explained by fundamentals" (Alexander, Pg. 12). The UK FSA, like CFTC Commissioner O'Malia, favor what they refer to as "position management" rather than "position limits" (Alexander, Pg. 12). The FSA believes that methods for "preventing (market) manipulation arising from large positions should include "a broad position management approach" because there is a lack of evidence showing that a "blanket approach through specific position limits" works (Financial Services Authority, Pg. 3132). The FSA stated that due to "the complex, disparate, and international nature of OTC markets, we (FSA) consider position limits to be unworkable on a marketwide basis (Financial Services Authority, Pg. 33).

The European Union (EU), on the other hand, although it seems to be supportive of position limits as a whole, has yet to "officially propose hard position limits"; and its progress is lagging behind that of the US, which could collectively pose challenges for the global financial industry and markets (Alexander, Pg. 12). The European Market Infrastructure Regulation (EMIR) started as a "directive" and changed to a "regulation"; therefore, all 27 Member States of the European Union must now enact it as law ("Euroccp"). The EMIR is the EU's equivalent to the US's DFA in purpose (i.e. improving transparency, enhancing regulatory oversight, mitigating aspects of the global financial crisis, etc.), however, EMIR is "part of a broader initiative to regulate market infrastructure in Europe that includes other pieces of legislation such as the Markets in Financial Instruments Directive (MiFID), which is currently under review in coordination with other regional and supra national financial regulatory elements and legislation (i.e. Capital Requirements Directive IV (Basel III), Central Securities Depository (CSD), etc.)—while being in line with principles put forth under the auspices of the G20 ("Euroccp"). French President

Nicolas Sarkozy supports position limits, and as the most recent President of the G20 held in Cannes, France, in November 2011; he made the issue of combating commodity price volatility as a Summit priority (Sarkozy, Pg. 3). CFTC Chairperson Gary Gensler has received support for position limits from EU Member States, and these governments have also called for position limits to be included in amendments to the UK's legislation—the Market Abuse Directive (MAD) (McGlinchey, Pg. 1).

In spite of the persistent disagreement throughout regulatory, legislative and public debate (as well as the diverging philosophy on the role and purpose of regulation, particularly when dealing with position limits in commodity futures and OTC markets) there is some light at the end of the tunnel. The paradox of trying to apply national regulations to a global market—that being the commodity futures and OTC derivatives, has provoked some potential for agreement. If there were potential for international consensus, it would be due to the fact that all important market actors complain about something referred to as "regulatory arbitrage". In the area of finance, "arbitrage" refers to the practice of taking advantage of a price difference between two or more markets in order to capitalize. The current debate surrounding this issue has led to a cause of concern for regulatory arbitrage, which basically means, that the market participants in this highly and increasingly global market, will simply pick up and go to where regulations are less strict and more lax, hence creating a financial regulatory "race to the bottom". Market participants based in the US often utilize this argument when lobbying against the DFA's more advanced regulations vis-à-vis the less advanced regulatory schemes of the UK, EU, Asia, etc.

The conclusion of a recently held "Regulatory Reform Summit 2011", organized by the trade association—Securities Industry and

Financial Markets Association (SIFMA), for instance, highlighted that "all panelists agreed (...) and stressed that any new (regulatory) rules must be aligned with international standards so as not to facilitate regulatory arbitrage" ("Securities Industry and Financial Markets Association"). In a testimony to the US Senate, Chairman of the International Swaps and Derivatives Association (ISDA), Stephen O'Connor expressed his concern by stating a concrete example that "if derivative transactions between an Italian company and UK subsidiary of a US bank were subjected to Dodd-Frank, but similar transactions between that Italian company and a UK bank (without a US parent) were not subject to those same rules, the end result would be that foreign companies would avoid doing business with swaps dealers affiliated with US companies" (Grant, Pg. 13). Both the industry and regulators agree these markets are global; and more so, they believe (or are at least learning as they address these new groundbreaking regulations that respond to the 2008 world financial crisis), that any national regulations must conform to the globality of the market.

Jean-Pierre Jouyet, Chairman of the France's regulatory authority Autorité des Marchés Financiers (AMF) calls for the "broadest possible enforcement" of regulation in order to avoid what he calls "regulatory shopping" (Jouyet, Pg. 8). Emphasizing the globality of this market, Jouyet stated "implementing a regulatory framework solely at the national level would have no impact on supervision of other commodity markets located in London, Chicago, New York, Switzerland, or Asia" (Jouyet, Pg. 8). The CFTC and US Securities and Exchange Commission (SEC), as two implementing agencies of the DFA, are aware of the international issues related to the implementation (of Title VII) of the DFA. Ethiopis Tafara, Director of the US SEC Office of International Affairs acknowledged that capital markets have always been global, but "it's the exponential advances in computer and telecommunication technologies that have altered the (global) dimension" ("US Securities and Exchange Commission", Pg. 14). Tafara highlighted the fact that "large banks and other financial institutions dominate the derivatives markets" and "55 to 75 percent of US banks' total exposure (as of 2008) to derivatives involved a counterparty resident outside the US" ("US Securities and Exchange Commission", Pg. 16).

William Dudley, President of the US Federal Reserve Bank of New York warned that "it is unlikely that the G20 countries will meet their goal of clearing all standardized OTC derivative trades through central clearing counterparties by the end of 2012" and that "cracks have started to appear between the US and Europe (…) on crossborder coordination" (Grant, Pg. 1). He cautioned, "regulatory oversight is national, but many financial firms and infrastructures operate on a global basis. Effective reform requires mutually consistent global standards, and while international cooperation to date has been good on many fronts, progress is uneven" (Grant, Pg. 2). Financial industry representatives and experts, addressing these international issues related to the DFA, highlighted key concerns and questions including: potentially "conflicting" multiple sets of rules applying to the same trader; "duplication", where applicable regulation elsewhere, should render you not subject to US regulation, the challenge of national regulation needing to be "comparable" across borders, duplicative trade reporting and the inability to "clear the same trade in two difference places"; the supposed "disadvantage of the US", due to the DFA coming into affect before other national regulatory schemes, etc. ("US Securities and Exchange Commission", Pg. 27-40).

In addition to issues of regulatory arbitrage and the inherent challenges of trying to apply national regulation to a global market, there is another challenge, which is: the market players are too powerful. We have heard of the concepts: "too 'big' to fail" or "too 'integrated' to fail"; well now we could also say we have "too-big-to 'regulate'"—meaning that under the current market conditions the new players (i.e. commodity index funds) are not only financially, technologically, intellectually, globally, and politically adept; but their power far surpasses that of any one government—even governments as large as the US. They are so powerful, and so convinced of their power, that they are even willing to take on the government, and its regulators, with legal action ("CFTC faces lawsuit over position limits rule"). They are so powerful, that Robert E. Litan of the Brookings Institution in Washington DC, refers to them as the "Derivatives Dealers' Club" that resists change to "derivatives market reform" (Litan, Pg. 08). Utilizing an example where CFTC Chairman Gary Gensler was asked at a gathering of major dealerbanks "what he saw as the biggest obstacles to derivatives reform"; he stated, Gensler's reply was "You" (meaning the banker-dealers) (Litan, Pg. 9).

The G20 Summit in Pittsburgh in September 2009, called for "improving the OTC derivatives markets and creating more 'powerful' tools to hold large global firms to account for the risks they take" (G20, Pg. 3). As of yet, this measure has not been fulfilled, the tools being created are not "powerful", and the global firms are still taking the same "risks" they took during the height of the global financial crisis. Therefore, not even the G20, the "premier forum for international economic cooperation" has been able to make progress on this measure, not to mention the fact that the G20 is also home to financial markets where these absurdly powerful commodity index investors reside (Bradford and Lim, Pg. ix). A more global, more institutional, and more legally binding international approach needs to be instituted. Although the G20 provides "strategic leadership" as a "steering committee" for the global economy; at the same time, it is limited by its informality, its lack of authority, its periodicity, its lack of representativeness, and its lack of institutionality (Bradford and Lim, Pg. 4).

Effective regulation requires an approach that harnesses past contributions of what the Pew Financial Reform Project and NYU Stern School of Business call the "alphabet soup" of regulatory reform (i.e. G20, BIS, EU, FSB, IOSCO, IMF) and keenly places them under one universal umbrella due to the magnitude and grand scale of this market and its potential to undermine humanity (Acharya, Pg. 71). In order to effectively implement a global regulatory scheme that is sustainable and durable, this must be done under the auspices of the United Nations, with the support of all 193 Member States. For the first time in history, the United Nations General Assembly has placed the issue of "excessive international financial market speculation and extreme price volatility of food and related commodity markets" as part of its agenda of work ("UN General Assembly, Second Committee"). Its Second Committee, which deals with Economic and Financial issues (as of the November 2011) has docketed draft resolution A/C.2/66/L.7, which calls for two important measures: requests the President of the 66th Session of the UN General Assembly (2011-2012), "to establish a special openended working group to promote an exchange (...) towards reducing excessive price volatility and speculation in food commodity markets, including derivatives such as futures and OTC transactions"; and designates the UN General Assembly's provisional agenda for the following year to include, as an official (sub) item under "macroeconomic policy questions" the issue of "excessive international financial market speculation and extreme price volatility of food and related commodity markets" ("UN General Assembly, Second Committee"). These global measures begin an adequate alignment of the global institutionality required to address the globality of commodity futures financial markets.

BIBLIOGRAPHY

Acharya, Viral, et al. Dodd-Frank: One Year On. New York: New York University (NYU) Stern School of Business & Centre for Economic Policy Research (CEPR), 2011.

Alexander, Niamh, Nassime Ruch-Kamgar, and Alim Shaikh. "Exchanges & Order Execution, Position Limits: Key Issues, Timing & Potential Impact". Keefe, Bruyette & Woods Specialists in Financial Services. New York, New York. 06 September 2011.

Bradford, Colin, and Wonhyuk Lim. Global Leadership in Transition: Making the G20 More Effective and Responsive. Washington DC: Brookings Institution Press, 2011.

"CFTC faces lawsuit over position limits rule." Reuters. 03 December 2011.

"CFTC Factsheet on Final Regulations of Position Limits for Futures and Swaps." Commodity Futures Trading Commission (CFTC), Office of Public Affairs. 18 October 2011. <http://www.cftc.gov/ucm/groups/public/@newsroom/documents/file/pl_factsheet_final.pdf>

"CFTC & SEC Public Roundtable to Discuss International Issues related to the Implementation of Title VII of the Dodd-Frank Act." US Commodity Futures Trading Commission (CFTC) and US Securities and Exchange Commission (SEC). 01 August 2011. <http://sec.gov/news/press/2011/2011151transcript.pdf>

Chancellor, Edward. Devil Take the Hindmost: A History of Financial Speculation. New York: Plume, 2000.

Chilton, Bart. "Regulatory Re-entry". Remarks to the Cadwalader Energy and Commodities Conference. Houston, Texas. 06 October 2011.

Das, Satyajit. Traders, Guns and Money: Knowns and Unknowns in the Dazzling World of Derivatives. London: Financial Times Press, 2010.

Dicker, Dan. Oil's Endless Bid: Taming the Unreliable Price of Oil to Secure Our Economy. New York: Wiley, 2011.

Dodd, Christopher, and Barney Frank. Dodd-Frank Wall Street Reform and Consumer Protection Act or HR 4173 [Kindle Edition]. 2010. Amazon.com. Mundus Publishing. 25 July 2010 <www.amazon.com/DoddFrankStreetConsumerProtectionebook/dp/B003XF1DW8>

Dunn, Michael. "History and Role of the US Futures and Derivatives Markets". Remarks at the 2011 UNCTAD Global Commodities Forum. UNCTAD, Geneva, Switzerland. 01 February 2011.

"European Market Infrastructure Regulation (EMIR)." EuroCCP. 22 July 2011 <www.euroccp.co.uk/leadership/faq_emir.php>

"Federal Register, Vol. 76, No. 17." Commodity Futures Trading Commission (CFTC). 26 January 2011: 47524777. <http://www.cftc.gov/ucm/groups/public/@lrfederalregister/documents/file/20111154a.pdf>

Financial Crisis Inquiry Commission (FCIC). Financial Crisis Inquiry Report. Washington DC: Financial Crisis Inquiry Report, 2011.

Gensler, Gary. "Implementing the Dodd-Frank Act". Remarks at the George Washington School of Law. Washington DC. 14 January 2011.

Gensler, Gary. "Bringing Oversight to the Swaps". Remarks at the 20th Annual Hyman P. Minsky Conference on the State of the U.S. and World Economics. Ford Foundation, New York, New York. 13 April 2011.

Gensler, Gary. "CFTC eager to clean up swaps market". Letter. Politico. 01 September 2011.

Gensler, Gary. "Closing Remarks on Position Limits". Statement of Support by Chairman Gary Gensler. CFTC Headquarters. Washington DC. 18 October 2011.

Gensler, Gary. "Featured Luncheon Speaker". Remarks before the Securities Industry and Financial Markets Association (SIFMA). New York Marriott Marquis. New York City. 07 November 2011.

Grant, Jeremy. "FTfm, Special Report on OTC Derivatives, Avalanche of Rulemaking Blocks Road to OTC Clarity." Financial Times. 01 August 2011: 1317.

Grant, Jeremy. "International Trading needs Global Oversight." Financial Times. 13 October 2011.

Greenberger, Michael. "Derivatives in the Crisis and Financial Reform." The Political Economy of Financial Crises, Oxford University Handbook. Eds. Gerald Epstein & Martin Wolfson. Oxford: Oxford University Press, 2011. (forthcoming).

Group of 20. G20 Leaders Statement: The Pittsburgh Summit. Pittsburgh, Pennsylvania, 2425 September 2009.

"History of the CFTC." Commodity Futures Trading Commission (CFTC). 26 November 2011 < http://www.cftc.gov/About/HistoryoftheCFTC/index.htm>

Johnson, Simon, and James Kwak. 13 Bankers: The Wall Street Takeover and the Next Financial Meltdown. New York: Pantheon, 2010.

Jouyet, Jean-Pierre. "The Financialisation of Commodity Markets: What are the Challenges for Regulators?". Closing address at the 2011 AMF (Autorité des Marches Financiers) Scientific Advisory Board Conference. Paris, France. 06 May 2011.

Kelleher, Dennis M. "Better Markets Comment Letter submitted to CFTC on Position Limits". CFTC Headquarters. Washington DC. 28 March 2011. <www.bettermarkets.com>

Litan, Robert E. "The Derivatives Dealers' Club and Derivatives Markets Reform: A Guide for Policy Makers, Citizens and Other Interested Parties". Brookings Institution Initiative on Business and Public Policy. Washington DC. 2010.

Masters, Michael W., and Adam K. White. "The Accidental Hunt Brothers, How Institutional Investors are Driving Up Food and Energy Prices." Masters Capital Management (2008): 158.

Masters, Michael W., and Adam K. White. "The 2008 Commodities Bubble, Assessing the Damage to the United States and its Citizens." Masters Capital Management (2009): 114.

McDonald, Robert L. Fundamentals of Derivatives Markets. Boston: Addison Wesley, 2008.

McGlinchey, Rob. "Gensler Urges Position Limits in Europe." Derivatives Intelligence. 16 March 2010.

O'Malia, Scott D. "Does the Commission (CFTC) Always Know Best?". Opening Statement by Commissioner Scott D. O'Malia: Open Meeting on Position Limits for Futures and Swaps; Derivatives Clearing Organizations; Effective Date for Swap Regulation. CFTC Headquarters. Washington DC. 18 October 2011.

O'Malia, Scott D. "Statement of Dissent, Position Limits for Futures and Swaps". CFTC Headquarters. Washington DC. 18 October 2011.

Pearlstein, Steven. "Steven Pearlstein: You Bet it's Another Bubble." The Washington Post. 04 November 2011.

"Regulatory Reform Summit 2011." Securities Industry and Financial Markets Association (SIFMA). 13 July 2011 <www.sifma.org/regreform2011>

Sarkozy, President Nicolas. "Keynote Address". Speech at European Commission Conference on Commodities and Raw Materials. Brussels, Belgium. 14 June 2011.

Soros, George. The Crash of 2008 and What it Means: The New Paradigm for Financial Markets. New York: Public Affairs, 2008.

"Speculative Position Limits." Futures Industry Association (FIA). 18 October 2011. <www.futuresindustry.org/positionlimits.asp>

UK Financial Services Authority (FSA). HM Treasury. Reforming OTC Derivative Markets, A UK Perspective. London: United Kingdom, December 2009.

United Nations Conference on Trade and Development (UNCTAD). Price formation in financialized commodity markets. Geneva, Switzerland: UNCTAD, 2011.

"United Nations General Assembly, Second Committee, Status of draft proposals." United Nations General Assembly. 01 December 2011. <http://www.un.org/en/ga/second/66/proposalstatus.shtml>

US Energy Information Administration (EIA). US Department of Energy (DOE). World Oil Balance 20042008. Washington DC: EIA, 2009.

CHAPTER 7
THE POLITICAL ECONOMY OF THE EUROZONE: GLOBAL GOVERNANCE'S GROWING PAINS

After more than five decades of efforts to unify Europe under one common political and economic umbrella, the current Prime Minister of the United Kingdom (UK), David Cameron, seems to be bearing the brunt for "backing out" (and not supporting) of what has been more commonly referred to as the "Treaty Summit", organized to negotiate a new European Union (EU) Treaty aimed to save the current EU and its single currency, the Euro. David Cameron, whose country has yet to adapt the single currency, would say "...what is on offer is not in Britain's interests, so I did not agree to it" (Lyall). On the other hand, others would believe that the UK, and other countries like it in Northern Europe, need to do more to save the idea of an integrated Europe, which could and should "drive forward (...) the pride of being an example of multilevel governance for the world to see, the extension of democracy, and the pooling of sovereignty that can make the years ahead an age of peace and prosperity" (Dervis and Özer, Pg. 225). The renowned Jean Monnet himself, known as the architect of European unity, said, however, that "the community (Europe) we have created is not an end in itself (...) (it is) only a stage on the way to the organized world of tomorrow (Dervis and Özer, Pg. 200).

But, before judging (or prejudging) Prime Minister David Cameron, it is important to understand that he, and those involved in the process of creating "the Europe" that Jean Monnet aspired to, are operating within the context of what Dani Rodrik refers to as the "political trilemma (of the world economy)" (Rodrik, Location 3042). Rodrik believes that globalization today possesses a "paradox", or what he refers to more succinctly as an "inevitable clash between politics and hyper-globalization" (Rodrik, Location 3096). Hyper-globalization in this case would be the process to consolidate (or specifically in the case of the Eurozone crisis "to save") the European monetary union, its Euro, and the EU itself.

The "politics" would correlate to local British politics and its intense debates regarding the Euro and the EU. The "trilemma" is defined by a relationship between three dimensions: hyper-globalization, democratic politics, and the nation state (Rodrik, Location 3313). To assume (or greater assume) one, you must give up the other(s). Prime Minister Cameron, in the case of recent deliberations on the "EU Treaty", decided to act in the interest of democratic politics and the nation state (that being Britain), by forfeiting his support for "hyper-globalization". The trilemma shows us that there exists a "fundamental tension between hyper-globalization and democratic politics" where "hyper-globalization (...) require(s) (the) shrinking (of) domestic politics and insulating technocrats from the demands of popular groups" (i.e. London-based financiers), particularly, if your desire is that of "deep (European) integration" (Rodrik, Location 3114).

The idea of European integration dates back to the days following World War II. In 1957, the European Economic Community (EEC) was created with the goal of establishing the "free movement" of "goods, capital, services, and people"; all of which made European-based "monetary fluctuations" potentially "more harmful" hence serving as a catalyst for "European monetary unification" (MourlonDruol, Pg. 2). In 1969, The Hague Summit, decided to "set up the Werner Committee in order to discuss European monetary unification", which had a lot to do with the affirmation of Europe as an "international actor", later becoming strongly related to questions of "European identity" (MourlonDruol, Pg. 3).

Today, however, the very survival of the Euro as a currency is in jeopardy. Therefore, the EU, as an example of multi-level economic governance, is at risk as well. French economist Jacques Rueff once said, "Europe will be made through a common currency or will not be made" (MourlonDruol, Pg. 6). French President

Nicolas Sarkozy declared, "the end of the euro would be the end of Europe" (MourlonDruol, Pg. 8). Although, not every member country of the EU is a member of the Eurozone—the EU has twenty-seven members and the Eurozone has ten, whereby some of the EU member countries including UK, Denmark, and Sweden decided not to join the Eurozone; although they did so in accordance with the EU Treaty provision, which says you "eventually" have to join (Dervis).

The EU member countries that assumed the Euro did so for three reasons: first, to reduce transaction costs and constant uncertainty (i.e. imagine if you had to exchange your US dollars for another currency every time you traveled outside your hometown, state, or province); two, to extend the European common market [i.e. you need a common currency to avoid risks to (trade related) profits and costs as a result of exchange rate volatility]; and three, to regionally share a monetary policy agent and borrow at the same rates [i.e. a shared European Central Bank (ECB)] (Dervis). The EU member countries that did not assume the Euro, did so for reasons, which include (but are not limited to): local politics, the desire to maintain the ability to unilaterally devalue the national currency and/or make national monetary policy by retaining their country's national Central Bank.

After the formation of the Euro, interest rates converged due to the decrease in currency risk now associated with forming part of the Eurozone. The risk of currency devaluation was eliminated, however, the risk of default on sovereign debt was still present. A good comparative example of this would be New York City's debt, which would not devalue because it is in US dollars, however, in the 1970s; New York City was on the verge of default (Dervis). EU interest rates also converged because market players could not imagine EU member countries defaulting on debt; because defaulting has normally been limited to developing countries of the non-European "third world", at least over the last fifty-to-sixty years (Dervis).

As a result of this convergence of interest rates, borrowing was made attractive, particularly for the newest EU members, those of which were more commonly referred to as the members of "the periphery", "the South", or "the Mediterranean". These countries, also known as PIGS (Portugal, Ireland, Greece, and Spain), although not all equally similar in this respect, began borrowing and borrowing, some (much) more than others; and as they continued to borrow, the more pressure they put on wages and prices (Mourlon-Druol, Pg. 9). And by lending to these countries at the same interest rates, as say The Netherlands, for example; loans were actually being made in real terms at lower rates (Dervis).

Wages, salaries, and prices in these periphery countries became "more aggressive" as such costs had a tendency to increase more in these countries vis-à-vis other economies of the Eurozone, particularly those to "the North" (i.e. Germany, The Netherlands, etc.) (Dervis). Additionally, these peripheral countries took on expansionary fiscal policy. Their national fiscal policies were "less tight" (Dervis). This created an increasing divergence inside the Eurozone in terms of costs (i.e. Italian unit labor costs went up for the same product by more than 25 percent vis-à-vis Germany, while those in Greece increased by up to 30 percent), which made these countries increasingly current account deficit countries, while northern countries ran current account surpluses (Dervis). Flassbeck considers the current crisis also a result of "Germany's wage dumping" (Crotty, Pg. 1). He believes "Germany pursued a policy of restraining their labor costs, which enabled the country to become extremely competitive against its euro partners"; and as such, Flassbeck argues that the current crisis is "inappropriately diagnosed as a budget deficit crisis and should instead be seen as a 'competitiveness gap' crisis" (Crotty, Pg. 1).

The fiscal policy of the periphery countries has become the pivotal point in the deliberations of the recent EU Summits as well as a contentious issue throughout the local politics of EU member countries. The alarms (of the crisis) were sounded when the market began looking at the debt to GDP ratios of said countries; which, for example, has Italy (Europe's fourth largest economy) at a debt to GDP ratio of 120 percent; or Portugal at 100 percent. In addition to the severe indebtedness, the other accompanying problem in this Eurozone crisis has become a lack of growth (Dervis). The fact that the cost structure in these economies has been increasing (i.e. up to 30 percent more than Germany), has meant that growth has been slowed down, hence making these economies uncompetitive (Dervis). Flassbeck stated, "the euro will not survive unless we tackle this (competitiveness) problem" (Crotty, Pg. 1).

Although the most recent efforts of EU member countries to solve this problem have focused (at least in the media) on UK Prime Minister Cameron's defection at the recent EU Summit this past December 2011, in favor of Britain's policy position; there have been positive steps made towards addressing the root causes of the crisis as well as its medium to long-term solution. The Brookings Institute underscored, on a more optimistic note, that the "correct road toward a solution to the European crisis has been taken", stating that, as a result of the recent EU Summit "all the necessary instruments are finally available: credible national leaders, adequate bailout funds, a legal and even judicial basis for a real fiscal union and quantitative credit easing", going as far to say that "should the emergency on the financial markets be contained, we will remember 09 December 2011, as a turning point for European history" (Bastasin, Pg. 1).

The most important aspect of the current Eurozone crisis seems to be that the EU member countries have a pretty good idea as to what needs to be done economically. Also, there seems to be close to a unanimous understanding that retreating from the Euro would be more costly than worth it. Following the recent EU Summit, the current ECB president, Mario Draghi, underscored this last point by arguing that "even if it were possible for countries to leave the Eurozone, it 'would not help'; currency devaluation would lead to inflation 'and at the end of that road, the country would have to undertake the same reforms (…) but in a much weaker position (…) (under) a substantial breach of the existing (EU) treaty" (Barber, Pg. 4). Not to mention, any unilateral decision to do so, would have an external effect on the other EU member countries. Consequently, the most probable outcome to current efforts to save the Euro will likely result in "neither (the Euro's) collapse nor a dash towards (it's) integration, but for the euro zone to muddle through" ("Europe's Future" Pg. 2). Therefore, every country's position and their efforts seem to be leaning in the direction that they want to make this work— either to stay as part of the European single currency or the EU.

The work towards a solution to the crisis and the consolidation of European integration will be strenuous, tedious, and mentally stressful. Why? Because the politics behind saving the Euro are culturally deep and incredibly complex. In 2007, Jean Claude Juncker, Prime Minister of Luxembourg, notably stated, "the barrier to (EU) reform has always been political, not economic (…) we all know what to do, but we do not know how to get reelected (in our own countries) once we have done it" ("Europe's Future" Pg. 3). Recently, in countries including Finland, Hungary,

Italy, the Netherlands, Germany, and the UK; populist leaders from opposition political parties have denounced the proposed EU Treaty changes agreed to at the December EU Summit, even though the agreement would strictly limit spending in signatory countries (Spiegel, Pg. 1). German chancellor, Angela Merkel, who defended the Summit's agreement, meanwhile had "a senior figure in the (German) Free Democratic party", a junior partner in her ruling coalition, resign amid a contentious party vote on the Euro's rescue plans" ("Doubts over Eurozone Deal", Pg. 1). In the Netherlands, political tensions are driven by angry voters; where "63 percent opposes any further aid to Greece (...) and 82 percent do not believe the government's assurances that Greece will pay the money (recent bailout package) back" (Steinglass, Pg. 1). Economist Jeffrey Sachs, stated after attending the G20 Summit in Cannes, France, (an event whose agenda was dominated by the problem of the Eurozone) this past November 2011, that "every leader involved in these (Eurozone) discussions is constrained by the need to address the concerns of his or her own electorate (Crotty, Pg. 2).

Part of the reason why democratic politics presents a challenge back home for European leaders is because of the ambiguous territoriality of Europe. No one really knows where Europe starts or where Europe ends. In addition to the aforementioned reasons as to why countries joined the Euro, it is important to mention that the primary aim behind the actual creation of the Euro was to garner political support for European integration. Countries knew there were concrete economic and political benefits to joining the European Economic and Monetary Union (EMU); which, in itself served as a catalyst for the creation of required political and legal frameworks. The Euro and the EU, helped to draw the lines of Europe, at least in terms of the "functions" and rules that went along with this global and regional governance entity.

Particularly, as the EU grew, however, its origins; and even the outcomes of the recent EU Treaty Summit, have grown increasingly "functional" in nature. The renowned British historian and political theorist David Mitrany, claimed that "territory" was the "old way" of determining membership in a "continental union" or "universal league"; while the more appropriate way (in determining membership), in terms of "integrating" those "with regard to the interests of all", was to define membership based upon "function" (Dervis). In the case of the EU, this "functionalist" approach helped to include new members during the EU's enlargement phase(s). Peripheral countries in the EU's south, along the Mediterranean; some of the same countries in economic trouble today; are considered part of Europe because of the "functions" of the EU.

On the other hand, author of the Clash of Civilizations and the Remaking of World Order, professor Samuel P. Huntington saw the world through an optical lens based upon civilizations that "share cultural affinities" (Dervis). Huntington believed the world should be divided into continental "superstates", rather than along a "functionalist" framework, because smaller countries had problems, and therefore, needed to turn to larger States for help (Dervis). In a "functionalist model, you can be a part of "multiple superstates"; however, in Huntington's model you are not able to serve as a member of two superstates (Dervis). Turkey is a key example, which has difficulties; because it is considered part of Europe, and also the Middle East, and even perhaps as an Arab State (Dervis).

Therefore, as a monetary union, similar to the monetary union of the United States; the question becomes, how does the EU generate the same type of "allegiance" to its "cultural identity"? How much allegiance do Europeans feel to the blue EU flag with yellow stars? Does (or does not) this allegiance (or lack of allegiance) compare to that of which American citizens share for the red, white, and blue US flag? How can Europe cultivate a "European identity" that is shared by all—both the EU member countries of the North as well as those of the South that were annexed during the enlargement process? These are important questions, and until they are answered, the political tension that European leaders are subjected to when they return home after EU Summits in Brussels and elsewhere will cease to subside.

Saving the Euro and consolidating European integration and the future of the EU is not going to be an easy task. There are deep and diverse cultural sensitivities all throughout Europe. For example, in France there is "great resentment about the dominance of the English language", so much so, that it has become "illegal to play too many English songs on the radio" ("Future of the EU"). Large popular groups of citizens throughout the EU "can be easily inflamed by insensitive decrees from Brussels, or by 'unfair' treatment by one country of another", where "disputes over budget deficits, over-spending, beef, lamb, asylum seekers, chocolate, Iraq, among others" are common, and not mere posturing. These convictions often represent "historical issues and profound resentments" ("Future of the EU").

The EU needs to continuously strive towards a goal where all its member countries and their citizens feel that the problems of one member country are the problems of all member countries and the solutions are of benefit to all—maybe not of equal benefit, but benefit to one, must have beneficial externalities for others, and be understood as such. The best way to make progress towards this goal is to bridge the "functionalist model" with the "cultural identity based approach" of Samuel Huntington. Neither of these two approaches alone will work for the EU; but a hybrid of the two must be taken into consideration if the EU is to ever become an increasingly harmonious place to live. To achieve a more integrated Europe, the EU member countries will need to improve by taking into account the political realities of Europe as well as its missing sense of identity. To do so, the EU member countries will need to do a few things.

First, there is a need to find a leader. Internationally, not many people know who represents Europe. Europe's leader should be as commonly known at the international level as the President of the United States. Perhaps, rethinking the current system of a six-month rotating leader would help to make effective leadership possible. In addition to the issue of EU leadership, the historic and revered Jacques Delors, three-time president of the European Commission and renowned French economist also believes that the Eurozone (itself) needs a "core of dirigiste powers to run Europe in a more political and less technocratic way" ("Europe's Future", Pg. 2).

Second, the origins of the EU show that Europe "wanted to overcome the images of the past and the fear of the 'other' (and) the emotions that had, again and again, led to war and even genocide" (Dervis, Pg. 220221). It is important to find the modern day "other". Times have change, and the "other", that served as an impetus throughout the beginnings of European integration has vanished. Europe needs to redefine the "us" and "them". Who is the "other" today? For example, the Community of Latin American and Caribbean States was recently inaugurated in Caracas, Venezuela. Also known as "CELAC", this regional entity represents the integration of all of Latin America and the Caribbean; States, including those from South and Central America, the Spanish and English speaking Caribbean, the political "right" and "left"—all came together to create this organization. Why? CELAC clearly defines the "other" of yesterday and the "other" of today. CELAC member countries are driven by their origin and history. This is the 200th anniversary of the independence of their countries, where all of them, except for the Dominican Republic, share their independence to a European power (i.e. Spain, Portugal, France, etc.). The "other" of yesterday was "Europe". The "other" of today is the "USA". CELAC specifically makes a point to not include the USA, Canada, Spain, and Portugal in its hemispheric union. Additionally, although it lacks a leader, as does Europe, some of its members do push the legend of the father of the Latin American independence movement, Simon Bolivar, as their spiritual leader and guiding light.

Third, to achieve a more integrated Europe, the EU member states and their citizens are going to have to come to grips with the fact that the European project will take time, patience, and continuous effort. The key current challenge is that the EU is experiencing a series of growing pains that are inherent to the global governance process; not to mention, most of which are common due to Europe serving as the premier example of multilevel governance—whose example the world observes closely. Moreover, when Europeans "fear for their jobs and their savings, when their governments and companies cannot easily borrow money, when banks fail, and the single currency trembles, then the European Union (faces) not just an economic crisis, but a political crisis, as well" ("Europe's Future", Pg. 1). However, as Jacques Delors once said, "crises always lead to a leap in EU integration" ("Europe's Future", Pg. 2).

Finally, taking these points into consideration, it is important that Europe not compare its monetary union to the monetary union of the US. For any European, particularly during these moments when popular groups at the local level reject the outcome and progress of the EU Treaty Summit process; it seems easy to look to the US as a better working example for which to aspire. The US, however, has similar problems with its monetary union. Although the US does not seem to have public rejection on a StatetoState basis regarding unequal distribution of budgetary allocation, it does have popular groups—and even States, such as Texas—motivated by its current Governor and presidential candidate—rejecting the industry and financial bailouts of the 2008 economic and financial crisis in the US. Furthermore, the US has always been a politically divided bipolar population, with strong differences between conservative Republicans and liberal Democrats— especially during the recent decades. It took the September 11, 2001; terrorist attacks on the World Trade Center in New York City to unite the US. It prompted American citizens to hang the US flag from home fronts all across smalltown America. It was then that the Republican president of the US, George W. Bush, had the highest approval rating and support of the US citizenry. Today, the US is increasingly divided again. A significant percentage of Americans even question whether their President is an American citizen himself, or whether he worships the religion he says he worships (i.e. Christianity). Many think and say the current US President, Barack Obama, is Muslim.

Whether the US has the US dollar as its single currency, or the EU has the Euro as its single currency, consolidating a sense of national identity is not an easy task. It is a task that requires political skillfulness and the ability of its leaders to harness a crisis for the betterment of their people. Politics is an important part of our democracy; and democracy is a process, not an event. The democratic process requires attention and effort. Perhaps, that is why Jean Monnet said that the EU is "not an end in itself" (Dervis and Özer, Pg. 200).

BIBLIOGRAPHY

Barber, Lionel, and Ralph Atkins. "Mario Draghi: Charged to Save the Euro." The Financial Times. 18 December 2011. <www.ft.com/intl/cms/s/0/ea01b8 6227da11e1a4c400144feabdc0.html#axzz1h2NM1mQY>

Bastasin, Carlo. "Eurozone Summit: Maybe Too Late, But Not Too Little." The Brookings Institute. 14 December 2011. <www.brookings.edu/opinions/2011/1213_euro_summit_bastasin.aspx>

Crotty, Ann. "Why the euro zone crisis defies resolution." IOL South Africa. 13 November 2011. <www.iol.co.za/business/international/whytheeurozonecrisisdefiesresolution1.1177064>

Dervis, Kemal, and Ceren Özer. A Better Globalization, Legitimacy, Governance, and Reform. Washington DC: Center for Global Development, 2005.

Dervis, Kemal. "Global Economic Governance (Reform Agenda and the Political Economy of Global Reform: The Case of the European Union)" Lecture. School of International and Public Affairs (SIPA). Columbia University, New York, New York. 28 November 2011.

"Doubts over Eurozone Deal Weigh on Euro." The Financial Times. 14 December 2011. <www.ft.com/intl/cms/s/0/baf3767c264611e185fb00144 feabdc0.html>

"Europe's Future, Can anything perk up Europe? Yes: the European Union will thrive if its leaders seize the moment in the same way they did 20 years ago." The Economist. 08 July 2010 <www.economist.com/node/16539326>.

"Future of the EU, Enlarged or Broken?" Global Change.com, Patrick Dixon. 09 December 2011. <www.globalchange.com/futureeurope.htm>

Lyall, Sarah, and Julia Werdigier. "In Rejecting Treaty, Cameron Is Isolated." The New York Times. 09 December 2011. <www.nytimes.com/2011/12/10 /world/europe/britainisolatedaftervetoingeurozonepact.html>

Mourlon-Druol, Emmanuel. "The Euro Crisis: A Historical Perspective." The London School of Economics and Political Science. June 2011. <www2.lse.ac.uk/IDEAS/publications/reports/SU007.aspx>

Rodrik, Dani. The Globalization Paradox: Democracy and the Future of the World Economy. New York: WW Norton & Company, 2011.

Spiegel, Peter, and Giulia Segreti. "Populist Parties gain from Uncertainty." The Financial Times. 14 December 2011. < http://www.ft.com/intl/cms/s/0/e07 9847a267011e191cd00144feabdc0.html>

Steinglass, Matt. "Eurozone crisis rocks Dutch government." The Financial Times. 21 December 2011. <www.ft.com/intl/cms/s/0/68a7d5b8e46311e0844d00144feabdc0.html>

CHAPTER 8

THE WORLD OUTGROWS KYOTO: A 20TH CENTURY AGREEMENT IN A 21ST CENTURY WORLD: HOW TO MAKE CLIMATE STABILITY WORK FOR THE GLOBAL PUBLIC GOOD

In 1992, US President George H.W. Bush and over 100 other Heads of State and Government as well as 172 governments and thousands of participants from the public and private sectors and civil society converged upon Rio de Janeiro, Brazil, for what was referred to as the Earth Summit ("Environmentalists Plan for 2012 Earth Summit"). This important UN conference put sustainable development centerstage globally and gave birth to the codification of environment and development, forests, biological diversity, and climate change ("Major Agreements & Conventions"). The latter was classified as the UN Framework Convention on Climate Change, also known as the UNFCCC ("UNFCCC"). Five years after, in December 1997, the UNFCCC was formally supplemented by the Kyoto Protocol, which was named after the Japanese city where the international environmental treaty's third Conference of the Parties was held ("Kyoto Protocol"). The first Conference of the Parties (COP), more commonly known as "COP", was held in 1995 in Berlin ("UNFCCC Meetings").

Most recently, the last three COPs—COPs 15, 16, and 17, held in Copenhagen, Cancun, and Durban, respectively; have become most controversial—mostly due to a series of geopolitical shifts as well as economic, social, and environmental changes and challenges that have overwhelmed the planet during the last decade and a half, particularly a series of financial crises and frequent natural disasters and extreme weather patterns ("UNFCCC Meetings"). In 2010, for example, over 100,000 lives were lost as a result of more than three hundred and forty-seven natural disasters, whose damages accrued to over US $304 billion (Abdulaziz Al-Nasser). The recent COPs seemingly have had mixed results, most of which have shown little progress towards the treaty's aim, as evidenced in the recent outcome of COP 17 held in Durban, South Africa, in December 2011.

Physicist and advisor to German Chancellor Angela Merkel and European Commission President Jose Manuel Barroso, Dr. Hans Joachim Schellnhuber, considered Durban's results by stating "You could write either one of two headlines: 'Breakthrough for a world climate treaty', or 'License to do nothing for another decade'" (Von Der Goltz). New York Times' environmental correspondent assigned to COP 17, John M. Broder coined the "conflicts and controversies" as "monotonously familiar" (Broder, 27 Nov. 2011, Pg. 1). He described COP 15 in Copenhagen; the last COP to have included numerous Heads of State and Government, such as US President Barack Obama, which "hoped to write a new, legally binding treaty covering all parties"; as a failure that "collapsed in acrimony and fingerpointing" (Broder, 10 Dec. 2011, Pg. 3). Regarding Durban's COP 17, Broder stated "every year they (COPs) leave a trail of disillusion and discontent, particularly among the poorest nations and those most vulnerable to rising seas and spreading deserts (…) they fail to significantly advance their own stated goal of keeping the average global temperature from rising more than 2 degrees Celsius, or about 3.6 degrees Fahrenheit, above preindustrial levels" (Broder, 10 Dec. 2011, Pg. 1).

Broder, however, does not deny the "dedication and stamina of the environment ministers and diplomats" who are the primary participants at the COPs, however, he believes that "maybe the task is too tall" for them, stating that the "issues on the table are far broader than atmospheric carbon levels or forestry practices or how to devise a fund to compensate those most affected by global warming" (Broder, 10 Dec. 2011, Pg. 1). Nick Robins, an energy and climate change analyst at the London-based HSBC bank, more or less coincided with Broder asserting that, "there is a fundamental disconnect in having environment ministers negotiating geopolitics and macroeconomics" (Broder, 10 Dec. 2011, Pg. 2). Broder believes the COPs play out "politics on the broadest scale" particularly "relations among Europe, the United States, Canada, Japan and three rapidly rising economic powers, China, India and Brazil" (Broder, 10 Dec. 2011, Pg. 2).

These three rapidly rising economic powers believe they should not foot the bill for climate stability by having to assume the costs attributed to reducing their carbon emissions as stipulated in the treaty; while the industrialized countries, including the US, Europe, and others (also known as Annex I countries in the treaty; explained below) enriched themselves by emitting carbon dioxide (CO_2) throughout the twentieth century's era of industrialization. On the other hand, Europe, along with many African and smaller nations, is adamant that "any future accord be legally binding" however, the US, China, India, and several other major emitters of greenhouse gases have attached some difficult conditions to participation in any mandatory agreement" (Broder, 08 Dec. 2011, Pg. 2).

The US is not a party to the Kyoto Protocol. It has refused to consider ratifying it because of what it calls "asymmetrical obligations". It says this because of the difference between the Annex I countries (i.e. industrialized countries) that have an obligation to reduce emissions under the treaty, versus the rest called nonAnnex I that do not have an obligation (Broder, 27 Nov. 2011, Pg. 2). After the recent Durban conference, the commitment of nations to the Kyoto Protocol turned for the worse. Support for Kyoto decreased now to only European Union member countries and a few others, particularly after Canada officially withdrew its support the day after the Durban conference ended (Lomborg). Earlier Russia and Japan declined their support for extending Kyoto as well (Lomborg).

The most challenging political impediment towards advancing progress has remained the standoff between the world's two leading emitters of carbon—the US and China. Some experts say the COP negotiation process has, year-after-year, been hijacked by the Ping-Pong game" taking place between these two giants (Broder, 7 Dec. 2011, Pg. 2). The impasse became more complicated as a result of China having recently emerged as the planet's largest emitter of CO_2 and the "world's biggest energy consumer" in 2010 (Swartz). Throughout the gridlock orchestrated by these two behemoths, China's argument has remained that "its rapid economic growth and persistent poverty of millions of its citizens" gives them reason to not be bound by "the same emissions standards as advanced industrialized nations" (Broder, 7 Dec. 2011, Pg. 1).

In spite of the individual country positions that exist during each COP, Victor believes these COPs are politically charged because CO_2 is a global problem. He states "emissions waft throughout the atmosphere worldwide", while needing "hundreds of years (...) for natural processes to remove most of (the) pollution", which encourages "every nation (to politically) evaluate the decision to cut emissions with an eye on what other big emitters will do since no nation, acting alone, can have much impact on the planetary problem" (Victor, Location 564). In terms of making progress towards the goal of Kyoto of stabilizing greenhouse gas concentrations in the atmosphere, the results have been dismal. In regards to building and achieving the needed political support for the accord, results have been less than optimal also, as displayed by the lack of agreement and heated COP debates. Lomborg states that climate negotiators for twenty years have "celebrated deals that have not panned out", most of which have, for the worse, been "promises that have been made (and) have had no impact on global CO_2 emissions" (Lomborg). He supports a serious reflection on the Kyoto negotiations and considers the last two decades of debate to have been similar to "flogging a dead horse" (Lomborg).

More talking will not change the impasse that exists amongst the world's leading powers—most of whom emit the majority of our planet's carbon. The reason being is that the structure of the Kyoto Protocol has been inadequate since its inception. Its structural problem encompasses inadequacies that are economic in nature, including the infamous "free rider" phenomenon, which seems to have progressively gotten worse due to the Kyoto Protocol's lack of "completeness" combined with the changes inherent in the global economy, particularly due to increased levels of economic growth and carbon emissions, demonstrated by large emerging and developing economies. The US's chief negotiator at the Durban COP, Todd Stern, stated, "climate is a classic global commons problem" (Broder, 27 Nov. 2011, Pg. 3). He emphasized that "each country needs confidence that others are acting (…) international cooperation is important (…) you can't rationally address this problem (climate) at the international level unless you get all the major economies, developed and developing, acting in a common system" (Broder, 27 Nov. 2011, Pg. 3).

Barrett addressed the issue of climate as a "classic global commons problem" by analyzing said issue with a "global public goods lens" (Kaul et al. Pg. 7). Global Public Goods (GPGs) are important to managing globalization and the goods and bads (or opportunities and challenges or benefits and costs) it presents. GPGs and managing globalization are mutually reinforcing because managing globalization "requires understanding and shaping the provision of GPGs so that all parts of the global public benefit" (Kaul et al. Pg. 2). In order to better understand GPGs, it is first important to decipher between public and private goods. The latter are associated with "clear property rights" (Kaul et al. Pg. 3). With private goods, someone could ask, "Who owns this good?" Public goods, on the other hand, are associated with the "public domain" (Kaul et al. Pg. 3). GPGs are public goods with "benefits" (or costs) that "extend beyond countries or regions, across rich and poor population groups, and even across generations (i.e. affecting both present and future generations) (Kaul et al. Pg. 3). A key (marketbased) condition of a private good is that its ownership could be transferred or denied, hence making private goods "excludable" or "rival" in consumption (Kaul, Grunberg, and Stern, Pg. 3). For example, others cannot enjoy a piece of cake, once it is consumed. The consumption of public goods, however, is not excludable to one person or rival in nature (Kaul, Grunberg, and Stern, Pg. 3). GPGs as compared to public goods (whether local or national, etc.), not only have "strong qualities of publicness", but also have benefits that are "quasi universal in terms of countries (i.e. covering more than one group of countries)", while extending to "people in several (preferably all) population groups" and "different generations (both current and future)" (Kaul, Grunberg, and Stern, Pg. 2-3).

Barrett believes that "climate change is the hardest problem the world has ever tried to address collectively" (Harris, Pg. 3). The reason managing climate change is difficult is due in part to the global magnitude of the problem. Managing climate change is managing globalization. Managing climate change and globalization is managing a GPG, however, neither of the three— whether climate, globalization, or GPGs—are managed in the context of some form of government, hence the reason why global governance fixtures dominate the governance part (as in the act of governing without formal global government) of climate change, globalization and GPGs. This is why, in the international sphere, where there is no government, the question is often raised "(then) how are (global) public goods produced?" (Kaul, Grunberg, and Stern, Pg. 12). The answer is not to rush and create a world government to manage globalization and its primary challenges (i.e. in the case of climate change). The provision of GPGs must be voluntary (Kaul et al. Pg. 308). The answer is to find a means of making global economic governance work for the efficient and equitable provision of GPGs. If done correctly, as Paul A. Samuelson states, "what seems like nobody's business becomes everybody's business" (Kaul et al. Pg. v).

Barrett utilizes the Montreal Protocol, which stipulates limits on ozone depleting substances such as chlorofluorocarbons (CFCs), as an example of the effective provision of a GPG vis-à-vis the Kyoto Protocol. Barrett believes, inter alia, that Montreal has succeeded because it has attracted almost full participation (Kaul et al. Pg. 216). The Montreal Protocol imposes "emission limits on every party", whereas the Kyoto Protocol, on the other hand, imposes "limits only on the so-called Annex I signatories (industrial countries and Europe's transition economies)" while the remaining countries, referred to as "non-Annex I parties (that is, developing countries) are not subject to emission limits (Kaul et al. Pg. 207). This division falls within the concept applied during environmental negotiations referred to as "common but differentiated responsibility", which the Kyoto Protocol uses "in the broad sense of taking into account national characteristics in order to achieve the convention's ultimate goal" (Kaul et al. Pg. 282). The concept, however, is used in the Kyoto Protocol in the "more restrictive sense of differentiating countries' quantified objectives for limiting and reducing emissions" (Kaul et al. Pg. 282). According to Blanchard et. al., said concept has led to "little concrete policy advice (...) on options for the possible inclusion of developing countries in future agreements on emission targets" (Kaul et al. Pg. 283).

This lack of completeness, full participation, and/or division between Annex I and non-Annex I signatory countries has created impediments to achieving the GPG of climate stability. These impediments relate to issues of cost and leakage. The total cost of reducing global emissions would be "higher" than if abatement (of CO2 emissions) were "more widely distributed" (Kaul, Grunberg, and Stern, Pg. 207). The lack of full participation causes "leakage". This is where emissions shift from "countries bound by the Kyoto ceiling" to other countries that are not, hence creating a situation where "global emissions may fall less than if limits were imposed on all signatories" (Kaul, Grunberg, and Stern, Pg. 207). The Kyoto Protocol, as a supposed means to achieving and providing the GPG of climate stability, does not seem fair and equitably shared or provided. Many countries are perceived (or would be perceived, if Kyoto were to be working) to be not fairly contributing to the full cost of achieving the GPG of climate stability. This is the common "free rider problem" in economics.

The free rider problem is common to the supply of GPGs in general. Meaning, it does not only happen with respect to climate stability. Since mid-eighteenth century economics, the free rider phenomenon has been frequently addressed (Kaul, Grunberg, and Stern, Pg. 6). Scottish philosopher and economist David Hume believed that "gaining the cooperation of a thousand citizens to jointly work for the common good would fail in the face of an individual's incentive to 'free himself' of the trouble and expense, and …lay the whole burden on others" (Kaul, Grunberg, and Stern, Pg. 6). Barrett states how the Montreal Protocol (vis-à-vis Kyoto) does well in deterring free riders by "restricting trade between signatories and nonsignatories (…) in substances covered by the treaty and in products containing them"; highlighting that "these sanctions were 'to stimulate as many nations as possible to participate in the (Montreal) protocol'" (Kaul, Grunberg, and Stern, Pg. 211-212).

This trade related incentive was also accompanied by other individuals' incentives, especially for the largest economies.

Each individual country cared about the Montreal Protocol's role in combating ozone layer's depletion because it is the ozone layer that "blocks biologically harmful ultraviolet radiation from reaching the Earth's surface (and) retarding plant growth (...) and other marine life (...) (while causing) cataracts, immune suppression, (and) skin cancers" (Barrett, Location 1042). The concrete individual incentive for the US to commit to the Montreal Protocol could be evidenced in the episode in August 1987, where "a month before the Montreal Protocol was adopted, US President Ronald Reagan had a skin cancer removed from the tip of his nose" (Barrett, Location 1053). Beyond these health and environmentally related incentive issues; economically, in 1990, the US Council of Economic Advisors arrived at the conclusion that the "cost of complying" with CO_2 reduction targets then would be thirty-five to one hundred and fifty times more than the cost of complying with the Montreal Protocol (Kaul, Grunberg, and Stern, Pg. 206).

Leakage, although it may seem similar to the free rider problem, is actually different. Leakage "can only arise where there is international trade" (Kaul, Grunberg, and Stern, Pg. 215). The problem of leakage can actually be avoided by "making sure that participation in an agreement is full" because then there will not be any "other countries to which production can relocate" (Kaul, Grunberg, and Stern, Pg. 215). The problem of leakage is constrained in the Montreal Protocol. Its prevalence in the Kyoto Protocol is an economic and political problem; and leakage was one of the reasons the "US Senate opposed the Berlin mandate" early on in the UNFCCC process (Kaul, Grunberg, and Stern, Pg. 215). These problems of Kyoto are grounded in its faulty design (Barrett, Location 1271). Altogether, Kyoto lacks incentives. Kyoto lacks the "carrots and sticks" (i.e. enforcement) enshrined in the Montreal Protocol (Kaul, Grunberg, and Stern, Pg. 216). The "less-than-full participation" problem is crucial, and needs to be overcome if climate stability, as a GPG that is "aggregate" in nature, is to be achieved and provided globally.

Additionally, Barrett points out that "emission limits covered by the Montreal Protocol are permanent, whereas those covered by the Kyoto Protocol run only until 200812" (Kaul, Grunberg, and Stern, Pg. 211). This presents a problem because "investments to reduce emissions involve projects with lifespans of twenty-five years or more", hence making "long-term investments (towards reduced CO_2 emissions) look less attractive" (Kaul, Grunberg, and Stern, Pg. 211). But, perhaps this problem (of a lack of permanence regarding emission limits) is the silver lining regarding how to arrive at an effective Kyoto that incentivizes and ensures climate stability as a GPG.

All countries (both Annex I and non-Annex I) have been affected by climate change in some form or other, whether it is the hurricanes that batter the southeastern portion of the US, or the flooding and rising coastline throughout China mainland. It is appropriate, therefore, to acknowledge that reducing the world's CO_2 emissions depends on the cumulative efforts of all countries, especially these two (Barrett, Location 164). The political and economic impasse, which has been omnipresent at the past three COPs, have most likely been due to Kyoto's faulty design (as a treaty), rather than the lack of political will (collectively) of the parties to said treaty.

Climate stability, as a goal of the Kyoto Protocol and process, needs to be approached differently. Climate stability needs to be looked at through a GPG lens. This means that countries need to "move beyond controlling bads", in this case CO_2 emissions; and "move towards providing goods", which would be helped by unleashing innovative technologies that generate environmentally and socially sustainable economic growth while simultaneously reducing the CO_2 emissions that burn up the planet and cause economic havoc, environmental degradation, and social devastation throughout countries at the local level (Kaul et al. Pg. 42).

Also, "international development aid" needs to change and move from the "traditional donor-recipient model" to a more "multilateral cooperative model", where "development is conceptualized as a problem of providing GPGs, rather than a direct transfer of resources (…) facilitating the pursuit of global cooperative goals" (Kaul, Grunberg, and Stern, Pg. 211). This paradigm shift would contribute to the "economics of public good provision" by determining "not only the potential gains from cooperation but also the degree of cooperation that can be sustained by the anarchic international system" (Kaul, Grunberg, and Stern, Pg. 216). Dervis believes that a similar approach would advantageously change the way in which development cooperation is currently fashioned. He asserts that assessing developing countries' efforts towards poverty reduction and climate change mitigation should be supported by official development assistance (ODA) as a newly enhanced version of global venture capital that would not only serve to assist developing countries on the receiving end, but also would benefit donor countries by contributing to the GPG of climate stability, which is in the interest of all countries (Dervis, Pg. 24).

Overcoming failure at the most recent COPs; and getting on track towards effectively addressing climate change will require, Broder believes, in the near future, a "fundamental remaking of energy production, transportation, and agriculture around the world", which he calls the "sinews of modern life" (Broder, 10 Dec. 2011,

Pg. 2). His point here alludes to the GPG lens approach and its shift towards providing goods rather than mitigating the bads. Revkin believes the "real-time demand for energy and economic vigor continues to trump long-term climate concerns". As a result he believes the COP process would benefit largely more from a "focus on finding ways to boost energy access" rather than the "pollution-style restrictions on carbon dioxide" (Revkin, 12 Dec. 2011, Pg. 1). He highlights Harvard Law School research, which proposes "invigorating the faltering climate treaty process by shifting the focus from confrontations over emissions to collaborative work encouraging access to modern energy choices" (Revkin, 12 Dec. 2011, Pg. 1). That same research underscores that "two decades of debate (on the UNFCCC) (…) have created a zero-sum game without opportunities for solving problems by creating mutual gains" (Revkin, 12 Dec. 2011, Pg. 1). It echoes the youth delegate at the recent COP in Durban, South Africa, who frustratingly stated to governments "You've been negotiating all my life" (Revkin, 10 Dec. 2011, Pg. 1). The most powerful support for this argument is displayed in the response to Revkin's repeated inquiry to the "Bush administration's climate treaty team", where the US responds affirmatively when he asks if the world would have been "better off" signing a "Framework Convention on [Energy] Technology Change back in 1992, instead of one on climate change" (Revkin, 10 Dec. 2011, Pg. 2).

The most important lesson we seem to have learned as a result of the limited progress of the Kyoto Protocol negotiations is a political one. Politically, the United Nations, particularly its Secretary-General Ban Ki-Moon should take a moment to seriously reflect on the recent COPs. Politically, he should end what does not work, especially if what the world has before it is broken. Do not spend political capital and resources on something that seems to be permanently derailed and running further and further off the tracks, especially as non-Annex I countries get stronger—both economically and geopolitically. Also, as one of the most pressing issues of our time, the Secretary-General should reflect on past issues of equal global importance. Almost all globally pressing issues required some sort of alternative forum, especially to achieve progress.

The Cuban Missile Crisis, probably the closest the world has ever come to immediate annihilation, required negotiation in "multiple fora". Perhaps climate stability can only be achieved with alternative fora? Perhaps, what is needed, is some sort of G20, which aims to break the immediate impasse, which really exists at the level of Sino-US relations. The world seems to have outgrown Kyoto. The changes of the global economy show us that we have before us a twentieth century agreement in the twenty-first century. In light of this situation, how could we ever make climate stability work for the global public good? The task on the table is too tall for Kyoto.

BIBLIOGRAPHY

Abdulaziz Al-Nasser, Nassir. "Before the International Conference on the HOPEFOR Initiative: Improving the Effectiveness and Coordination of Military and Civil Defense Assets for Natural Disaster Response." Speech. President of the 66th Session of the UN General Assembly, Doha, Qatar, 27-29 November 2011. <www.un.org/en/ga/president/66/statements/hopefor291111.shtml>

Barrett, Scott. Why Cooperate? The Incentive to Supply Global Public Goods. New York, New York: Oxford University Press, 2010.

Broder, John M. "At Meeting on Climate Change, Urgent Issues but Low Expectations." The New York Times. 27 November 2011. <www.nytimes.com/2011/11/28/science/earth/nationsmeetto addressproblemsofclimatechange.html>

Broder, John M. "At Climate Talks, a Familiar Standoff Between U.S. and China." The New York Times. 07 December 2011. <www.nytimes.com/2011/12/08/science/earth/atclimatetalksafamiliar standoffemergesbetweentheunitedstatesandchina.html>

Broder, John M. "US Climate Envoy Seems to Shift Stance on Timetable for New Talks." The New York Times. 08 December 2011. <www.nytimes. com/2011/12/09/science/earth/usclimateenvoyseemsto shiftpositionontimetablefornewinternationaltalks.html>

Broder, John M. "In Glare of Climate Talks, Taking On Too Great a Task." The New York Times. 10 December 2011. <www.nytimes.com/2011/12/11/science/earth/climatechange expandsfarbeyondanenvironmentalissue.html>

Dervis, Kemal. "WIDER Annual Lecture 11, The Climate Change Challenge." Lecture. United Nations University World Institute for Development Economics Research (UNUWIDER). Helsinki, Finland. 2008.

"Environmentalists Plan for 2012 Earth Summit." Worldwatch Institute. 16 December 2011. <www.worldwatch.org/node/6286>

Harris, Richard. "Ahead Of Climate Talks, U.S. Leadership In Question." National Public Radio. 28 November 2011. <www.npr.org/2011/11/28 /142714839/ aheadofclimatetalksusleadershipinquestion>

Kaul, Inge, Isabelle Grunberg, and Marc A. Stern. Global Public Goods, International Cooperation in the 21st Century. New York, New York: Oxford University Press, 1999.

Kaul, Inge, et. al. Providing Global Public Goods, Managing Globalization. New York, New York: Oxford University Press, 2003.

"Kyoto Protocol." UN Framework Convention on Climate Change (UNFCCC). 16 December 2011. <unfccc.int/key_documents/ kyoto_protocol/items/ 6445.php>

Lomborg, Bjørn. "The Emperor's New ClimateChange Agreement." Opinion-Editorial. Project Syndicate. 10 January 2012. <www. projectsyndicate.org/commentary/lomborg80/English>

"Major Agreements & Conventions." United Nations Department of Economic and Social Affairs (DESA), Division for Sustainable Development (DSD). 16 December 2011 <www.un.org/esa/dsd/ resources/res_majoagreconvover.shtml>

Revkin, Andrew C. "Dot Earth, Young Voices Reverberate at Indeterminate Climate Talks." The New York Times. 10 December 2011. <http://dotearth. blogs.nytimes.com/2011/12/10/youngvoicesatdeadlockeddurbanclimatetalks>

Revkin, Andrew C. "Dot Earth, A Post-Pollution Path to Global Climate and Energy Progress." The New York Times. 12 December 2011. <http://dotearth. blogs.nytimes.com/2011/12/12/apostpollutionpathtoglobalclimateandenergyprogress>

Swartz, Spencer, and Shai Oster. "China Tops US in Energy Use, Asian Giant Emerges as No. 1 Consumer of Power, Reshaping Oil Markets, Diplomacy." The Wall Street Journal. 18 July 2010. <online.wsj.com/article/ SB10001424052748703720504575376712353150310.html>

"UNFCCC Meetings." UN Framework Convention on Climate Change (UNFCCC). 16 December 2011. <unfccc.int/meetings/items/6240.php>

"UNFCCC." UN Framework Convention on Climate Change (UNFCCC). 16 December 2011. <http://unfccc.int>

Victor, David G. Global Warming Gridlock: Creating More Effective Strategies for Protecting the Planet. New York, New York: Cambridge University Press, 2011.

Von Der Goltz, Jan. "Durban Climate Deal: What a Great Result This Would Have Been Some Ten Years Ago!" Global Development: Views from the Center (Blog). Center for Global Development (CGD). 13 December 2011. Web. 16 December 2011. <http://blogs.cgdev.org/globaldevelopment/2011/12/durbanclimatedealwhatagreatresultthiswouldhavebeensometenyearsago.php>

CHAPTER 9

SEOUL TO CANNES: THE EVOLUTION OF A G20 AND A G-ZERO

The first four G20 Summits were held in G7 countries. The US was home to the first and third Summits, which were held in Washington DC in November 2008, and Pittsburgh in September 2009; while the UK and Canada hosted the second and fourth Summits, which were held in London in April 2009, and Toronto in June 2010, respectively ("G20 Summits"). The fifth G20 Summit was held in Seoul, South Korea. Because South Korea is not a G7 country, this was considered a major breakthrough for G20 countries, particularly for those economically emerging members. The Seoul Summit was also significant because it was organized in "tandem with the Asia Pacific Economic Cooperation (APEC) leaders' meeting", which took place immediately following the Seoul Summit in neighboring Yokohama, Japan (Kirton, Pg. 1). The Seoul Summit also made a unique effort to include civil society in the G20 deliberations by hosting a parallel business summit, a pre-summit scholarly conference, and a meeting of G20 parliamentarians (Kirton Pg. 2).

The G20's Washington DC Summit, held during the peak of the global crisis in 2008, situated the G20 as a "global crisis responder". This was the case throughout most of the following Summits. South Korea, however, the host country of the Seoul Summit made a noteworthy contribution to the G20 by furthering the Group's transition from "global crisis responder" to "global steering committee" (Bradford and Lim, Pg. 14). This transition was particularly critical because the Pittsburgh Summit declared the G20 the "premier forum for international economic cooperation" (Bradford and Lim, Pg. ix). More specifically, South Korea, transitioning the G20 from its crisis oriented role, placed the issue of development on the G20's work agenda for the first time. South Korea's credibility in the area of development, particularly due to its own development success achieved over the last generation, is unprecedented. South Korea's development model is reputed for its "focus on education, infrastructure, and the synergy between government and the private sector" (Bradford and Lim, Pg. 13).

South Korea understood the importance of exemplifying leadership throughout the year leading up to the actual Seoul Summit; and although it was keen on leading a successful Summit, the authorities were most likely aware that a successful Summit is not always an easy feat. South Korea was challenged with making sure that the G20 remained an "enduring body" (Bradford and Lim, Pg. 2). The G20 was in jeopardy of "fad(ing) away as a significant forum for global leadership as the global financial crisis subsid(ed)" (Bradford and Lim, Pg. 2). Additionally, the G20's dilemma has been the question of a "trade-off between achieving legitimacy as a representative body and achieving legitimacy as an effective body" (Bradford and Lim, Pg. 3). Part of the G20's purpose, however, is to provide for a forum where a smaller amount of countries could resolve their problems expeditiously without having to struggle to achieve agreement amongst a larger group of countries, such as the 193 Member States of the UN General Assembly, for example. A sizable majority of the nonG20 countries challenge this notion, however, and believe the G20 "has a representativeness deficit" (Bradford and Lim, Pg. 3). Also, at the time of the Seoul Summit; the G20 and South Korea—as the host country, were challenged with a "concern for leadership and communication" (Bradford and Lim, Pg. 3). South Korea had to make for a successful Summit, while confronting a "crisis of confidence in markets (...), a crisis of faith in the capacity of domestic and international institutions (...)", and a need to "restore public trust in national and global political leadership" (Bradford and Lim, Pg. 3).

In addition to its initial achievements, the Seoul Summit also ended positively. The Seoul Summit was also beneficial for having "delivered ahead of time on the Pittsburgh (Summit's) commitment to reform IMF governance, with a reform that shifted 6 percent of quota shares toward underrepresented countries", as well as, for having addressed "new financial safety nets", and taking "stock of an agreement reached in the Basel Committee to revise bank capital adequacy ratios" (Angeloni, Pg. 16). In spite of these steps forward, South Korea was confronted by some age-old stalemates, which Brazilian Finance Minister, Guido Mantega then referred to as a "currency war" (Angeloni, Pg. 15). Minister Mantega was alluding to the "currency dispute between the US and China", which was still alive and vibrant, as well as, a source for concern and disagreement at the highest levels of the G20. Although some sort of progress was made towards finding a compromise between China and the US regarding this issue, which included a statement that "current account balances should remain below 4 percent of GDP"; no agreement was achieved in time for the Seoul Summit, and the gridlock between two of the world's largest economies was passed off to the following G20 Summit, which was held in Cannes, France, in November 2011 (Angeloni, Pg. 15).

French president Nicolas Sarkozy was ambitious. France, as the host country for the 2011 G20 Summit, stocked the agenda with several issues. Earlier that year, numerous G20 ministerial meetings and seminars took place that addressed issues including "reform of the International Monetary System, strengthening financial regulation, combating commodity price volatility, supporting employment and strengthening the social dimension of globalization, fighting corruption, and working on behalf of development ("Priorities of the G20 French Presidency"). By mid-2011, however, the focus of the policy discussions of the Cannes Summit turned exclusively towards the issue of the Eurozone sovereign debt crisis (Angeloni, Pg. 20).

Although Kirton believed the Cannes Summit was "a summit of substantial success", particularly because, according to him, G20 leaders "(rode) to the rescue of a European Union that had tried but failed repeatedly to cope on its own"; other critical authority figures on the G20 came with a different perspective (Kirton, Pg. 1). Others believed the "outcome of Cannes fell dramatically short of expectations" (Angeloni, Pg. 20). Lee Dong-hwi , for example, went so far as to state that the "high expectations for the G20 had been lowered after the Cannes Summit" as a result of the "reduced effectiveness of the forum (Summit) and the absence of genuine leadership" (Dong-hwi , Pg. 1). He considered that "G20 leaders drew a blank in resolving the Eurozone crisis, due to disagreement between European countries, the political turmoil in Greece, the economic crisis in the US" as well as the "reluctance of China and other developing nations to intervene" (Dong-hwi, Pg. 1).

Dong-hwi believes the Cannes Summit was the most significant representation of an "absence of leadership" in all of the previous G20 Summits (Dong-hwi , Pg. 1). The lack of progress demonstrated by the Cannes Summit, he believes, is a result of what he calls "passive avoidance", where disagreements between the US and EU, between the US and China, and among the EU countries themselves, all held back progress (Dong-hwi , Pg. 2). Concretely, the setbacks at the Cannes Summit were due to, but not limited to: leaders failing to make significant progress on the French Presidency's priorities (those that ministers had been working on throughout 2011); no substantive conclusion on possible improvements to the International Monetary System, no progress on IMF surveillance or on managing volatile capital flows (Angeloni, Pg. 2021). There was also no real substance to the new "Action Plan for Growth" that was rolled out either (Angeloni, Pg. 21).

Grevi highlights that the Cannes Summit "did not show the same resolve to address the economic crisis" as did the G20 Summits in Washington DC and London in 2008 and 2009, respectively (Grevi, Pg. 1). While the US-born 2008 crisis left G20 members feeling they were "in the same lifeboat in the midst of a storm, facing clear and present danger" and "collective action (albeit via nationally determined policy packages) (as) the only option for collective survival"; the Eurozone crisis, on the other hand, was different (Grevi, Pg. 2). The response to the 2008 crisis was "driven by American leadership and convening power, with the strong initiative and support of the UK and France" (Grevi, Pg. 34). The Eurozone crisis did not even count on EU member states showing up at the Cannes Summit with a "common front" (Grevi, Pg. 34). The political will to confront the crisis "together", which did emerge from the Washington and London G20 Summits, was "not replicated in Cannes" (Grevi, Pg. 2).

The lack of progress at the Cannes Summit leaves the G20 at crossroads in terms of global economic governance. First, the failure of the Summit to make progress on priorities put forth by the French Presidency demonstrates a weakness of the G20 as a "global steering committee". Second, the failure of the Summit to make progress on the Eurozone crisis demonstrates a weakness of the G20 as a "crisis responder". Together, these two impediments, according to Grevi, make the G20 "neither a steering board, nor a crisis management committee"; and because of this, he predicts that the G20 has "entered an identity crisis" (Grevi, Pg. 2). Even before the Cannes Summit, the "legitimacy" of the G20 was questioned. This undermined legitimacy will continue to serve as a hurdle for leading Summit host countries, especially if the Summits take place while there is an absence of a global "sense of urgency to deal with a global crisis".

These problems that emerged as a result of Cannes, combined with the lack of progress on "global rebalancing", particularly related to the global imbalance at the level of the US and China, stands to seriously undermine the G20 as a premier forum of global economic governance.

Global imbalances have been a subject of debate, particularly since the Pittsburgh Summit (Rickards, Location 2115). In the case of the US and China, almost no progress whatsoever has been made concerning the global imbalance that exists between them, which according to the US, is fueled by China's artificially devalued currency. In 2010, however, shortly following the Pittsburgh Summit, China did allow its currency to "appreciate slightly" in value (Rickards, Location 2151). China most likely allowed this to happen in order to forestall being "branded a currency manipulator by the US Treasury, which could lead to trade sanctions by the US Congress" (Rickards, Location 2151). Global imbalances basically refer to the deficits and surpluses in the current accounts of countries vis-à-vis other countries (Bradford and Lim, Pg. 125). Addressing these imbalances, known as "rebalancing", requires a process of continued "macroeconomic policy adjustment" as well as "structural reform in both surplus and deficit countries"; with "exchange rates and budget deficits" remaining as an important part of G20 discussions, particularly because the issue of the US and China, for example; although seemingly bilateral in nature, has global ramifications (Wonhyuk and Nicolas, Pg. 17). Dervis, however, believes "it is important not to reduce the global rebalancing problem entirely to a problem between the US and China (Bradford and Lim, Pg. 130). He alludes to the important fact that global imbalances also exist in "many emerging market countries—including India, South Africa, Brazil, and Turkey" all of whom "actually run current-account deficits" (Dervis, Pg. 1). The Seoul and Cannes Summits addressed the global imbalances present throughout the global economy, while little progress was made at either Summit.

The Cannes Summit's lack of progress combined with the G20's struggle to gain global legitimacy highlights what Bremmer and Roubini call a "G-Zero world" (Bremmer and Roubini, Pg. 1). They believe that we live in a G-Zero world, rather than a G20 world because "the expanded group of leading economies has gone from a would-be concert of nations to a cacophony of competing voices as the urgency of the financial crisis has waned and the diversity of political and economic values within the group has asserted itself" (Bremmer and Roubini, Pg. 1). To support their argument they state that while "the US lacks the resources to continue as the primary provider of global public goods", other nations, such as the EU and Japan have "(no) time, resources, or domestic political capital" for what they refer to as "a new bout of international heavy lifting" (Bremmer and Roubini, Pg. 1).

Furthermore, Bremmer and Roubini agree that "no credible answers to transnational challenges" can be reached "without the direct involvement of emerging powers such as Brazil, China, and India"; however these countries, they believe, "are far too focused on domestic development to welcome the burdens that come with new responsibilities abroad" (Bremmer and Roubini, Pg. 1). Rodrik agrees with Bremmer and Roubini. He believes we are currently experiencing, what he refers to as, "leaderless global governance" (Rodrik, Pg. 1). His examples include the US and the EU, both of which are "now burdened by high debt and low growth" and therefore "preoccupied with domestic concerns" and "no longer able to set global rules"; while "rising powers such as China and India place great value on national sovereignty and non-interference in domestic affairs", hence "mak(ing) them unwilling to submit to international rules (or to demand that others comply with such rules)–and thus unlikely to invest in multilateral institutions, as the US did in the aftermath of World War II" (Rodrik, Pg. 1). The G20, although it has been overshadowing the G7 in the realm of global economic governance, seems to be doing so, however, more as a G-Zero than a G20. The future of the G20 depends not so much (about) who is rising in power or who is in relative decline; but rather who is prepared to "provide leadership and take risks to enable collective action, beyond short-term posturing and interest-maximizing considerations" (Grevi, Pg. 5)

BIBLIOGRAPHY

Angeloni, Ignazio. "The Group of 20: Trials of Global Governance in Times of Crisis." Bruegel. December 2011. <www.bruegel.org/publications/publicationdetail/view/655>

Bradford, Colin, and Wonhyuk Lim. Global Leadership in Transition: Making the G20 More Effective and Responsive. Washington DC: Brookings Institution Press, 2011.

Bremmer, Ian, and Nouriel Roubini. "A G-Zero World: The New Economic Club Will Produce Conflict, Not Cooperation." Foreign Affairs. Volume 90, Number 2 (March/April 2011).

Dervis, Kemal. "Global Imbalances and Domestic Inequality." Op-Ed. Project Syndicate. 10 January 2012. <www.projectsyndicate.org/commentary/ dervis6/English>

Dong-hwi , Lee. "Cannes G20 Summit: Assessment and Implications." The Institute of Foreign Affairs and National Security, Ministry of Foreign Affairs and Trade, Republic of Korea. December 2011. <www.g20.utoronto.ca/biblio/LEE620111212en.pdf>

"G20 Summits." G20 Information Centre, Munk School of Global Affairs at the University of Toronto. 16 December 2011 <www.g20.utoronto.ca/summits /index.html>.

Grevi, Giovanni. "The G20 after Cannes: An Identity Crisis." Fundación para las Relaciones Internacionales y el Diálogo Exterior (FRIDE). November 2011. <www.fride.org/publication/962/theg20aftercannes:anidentitycrisis>

Kirton, John. "A Summit of Substantial Success: The Performance of the Seoul G20." Munk School of Global Affairs at the University of Toronto. November 2010. <www.g20.utoronto.ca/analysis/kirtonseoulperf101113.html>

Kirton, John. "Cannes 2011: A Summit of Substantial Success." Munk School of Global Affairs at the University of Toronto. November 2011. <www.g20.utoronto.ca/analysis/111104kirtoncannesperf.html>

Kwan Yuk, Pan. "LatAm currencies: war again?" The Financial Times. 07 February 2012. <http://blogs.ft.com/beyondbrics/2012/02/07/latamcurrencieswaragain>

"Priorities of the G20 French Presidency." G20G8 France 2011. 16 December 2011. <www.g20g8.com/g8g20/g20/english/prioritiesforfrance/theprioritiesofthefrenchpresidency/theprioritiesofthefrenchpresidency.75.html>

Rickards, James. Currency Wars: The Making of the Next Global Crisis. New York: Penguin, 2011.

Rodrik, Dani. "Leaderless Global Governance." OpEd. Project Syndicate. 13 January 2012. <www.projectsyndicate.org/commentary/rodrik66>

Wonhyuk, Lim, and Françoise Nicolas. "The G20 from Seoul to Cannes: Towards a Global Governance Committee." Center for Asian Studies, Institut Français des Relations Internationales (IFRI). April 2011. <www.ifri.org/?page=contributiondetail&id=6528&lang=uk>

PART III
POLITICAL ECONOMY

CHAPTER 10

A REVIEW OF INTER-AMERICAN RELATIONS SINCE THE BEGINNING OF THE COLD WAR: A COMPARATIVE PERSPECTIVE FROM JUAN BOSCH TO CELAC

On December 3, 2011, thirty-three Heads of State and Government, representing both the Spanish and English speaking Latin American and Caribbean countries of the hemisphere, gathered in Caracas, Venezuela, for the Summit of the Community of Latin American and Caribbean States, also known for its acronym as CELAC. This Summit gave birth to this same Community ("CELAC"). The CELAC initiative was proposed oneyear earlier at the region's Rio Group Summit and the Latin American and Caribbean Summit on Integration and Development (CALC), both of which took place back-to-back in February 2010, under the auspices of the "Summit for Latin American and Caribbean Unity", in Riviera Maya, Mexico ("Cumbre de la Unidad").

As with many international endeavors in the region over the past several decades, the creation of the body provoked diverging opinions and strong criticism from opposite ends of the spectrum; while also gaining significant media attention (the majority of which was global media rather than US-based) due to the group's membership; however, not for who it included, but rather for who it did not include (i.e. US, Canada, Spain, and Portugal), all of whom normally participate and play a role in Western Hemispheric Summits and regional organizations such as the Organization of American States (OAS).

The host president of the 2010 Summit for Unity, Mexican president Felipe Calderón, said that CELAC proves that the dream of Simon Bolivar (who led Latin America's successful struggle for independence from the Spanish Empire over two centuries ago) for a united America "is more alive than ever". CELAC's 2011 host president, Venezuelan president Hugo Chavez said that CELAC will be "the most important political event to have occurred in our America in 100 years or more" (Keller). Cuban President Raul Castro, whose country's membership in the OAS was suspended in 1962, considered the creation of CELAC, "(if successful) to be the biggest event in 200 years" (Rueda).

On the other hand, Andres Oppenheimer, Latin American editor for the Miami Herald newspaper was pessimistic. He believes CELAC "will hardly make it into history books" and that it "will have no teeth" (Oppenheimer). Tim Padgett of Time.com Latin America considers the aspect of "Latin American integration" enshrined in CELAC to be "elusive, if not quixotic" (Padgett). Michael Royster, contributor to the Rio Times, criticized CELAC for its lack of substance highlighting that it has "yet to draw up statutes saying what it will do and how it will do it" (Royster). But, while Royster categorized the Summit's participants as "the usual left leaning luminaries", the Summit did include the participation of all thirtythree countries as well as almost every Head of State in the region, both from the left and right; most of whom, took a positive or objective stance regarding CELAC's work and perception (in ideological terms) and any potential reverberations (as a result of the latter).

Chile's center-right president and former businessman, Sebastián Piñera, who assumed the protempore presidency of CELAC for 2012, closed his remarks at the Summit in Caracas by emphasizing, "unity is the road ahead" stating that "a lot of people think that you can be faster when you move alone, but the truth is that together we will come much further" (Ebeling). Uruguay's leftist president and former guerrilla fighter, José Mujica coined CELAC a "second independence for Latin America", but cautioned that CELAC must be done "without falling into dogmatism and with inclusion and with respect for all, be it from the right, center or left" ("Mujica calls CELAC").

In order to understand the significance of CELAC, it is important to take a look back into history throughout the decades following

World War II and determine what precepts have guided (or did not guide) or have dominated Inter-American relations since the start of the Cold War. Two precepts that must be considered include: first, that an entity—whether it be a foreign government regime (i.e. foreign to the US); or a regional entity (as in the case of CELAC)—is (or are) often deemed either "pro-American" or "anti-American" (especially in the Cold War era and seemingly today also, according to sources); and second, that these same entities are often deemed either of the "left" (i.e. "the usual left leaning luminaries") or of the "right".

First, in the case of "anti-Americanism" versus "pro-Americanism", it is prudent to revise the contents of the aforementioned article by Andres Oppenheimer. Oppenheimer's thesis (in this article) was that CELAC stands to be a "new Latin American group that will 'have no teeth'" (Oppenheimer). He based this assertion, not only on the mere fruits of what looks like two interviews, one with "top US officials" and another with "Chilean Foreign Minister Alfredo Moreno", but also on the fact that these interviewees believe and equate CELAC's effectiveness to whether or not it will become an "anti" or "pro" American organization (Oppenheimer). Worse, Oppenheimer's analysis is based upon comparing "institutional effectiveness" vis-à-vis "anti-Americanism" by highlighting three reasons that pre-judge CELAC as an "ineffective tool for the region's economic integration" grounded in a rationale that has little or nothing to do with being in favor of or against America (Oppenheimer).

It is, however, quite possible that Oppenheimer views CELAC, more according to his own personal bias, which could quite considerably be that he believes CELAC to not be genuinely an "institution of (or for) Latin American integration", but more so a vehicle for the "anti-American" sentiments and political theater of President Hugo

Chavez—perhaps because the Summit was held in Caracas and chaired by President Chavez himself. In fact, Oppenheimer's third point (supporting why CELAC will be "ineffective") states "unlike a few years ago, when oil prices were high and Chávez was giving away petrodollars throughout the region, there is little appetite in most of Latin America for embracing an anti-American agenda" (Oppenheimer). This is not the issue, nor is it the motive for attending the CELAC Summit or supporting its ideals. It seems that Oppenheimer confusingly assumes or equates some relationship between past Petro-Caribe Summits of President Chavez with this inaugural CELAC Summit.

At any rate, yes there was some "anti-American" sentiments being voiced around the CELAC Summit floor during its two days of proceedings in Caracas, however, the majority of these statements, which were far and few between; where limited to the usual suspects including President Chavez himself, Cuban President Raul Castro, Bolivian President Evo Morales, among a few others. This, however, does not mean that the Summit or the CELAC as an institution for future Latin American integration was "anti-American", nor does it mean that any country that participated in this Summit was also individually in itself "anti-American". Even President Chavez, the ring-leader, when it comes to "anti-American" sentiments, could be considered to have been playing a game of "political theater", which could be considered of marginal importance when compared to the primary reasons behind why CELAC came to fruition.

For example, Romero and Corrales refer to President Chavez's antics as an act of "soft balancing" (Romero and Corrales, Pg. 219). They define soft balancing as "a country's efforts—short of military actions—to frustrate and undermine the foreign policy objectives of other more powerful nations" where it differs from "more traditional forms of 'power balance' in that the challenging nation seeks not to destroy the hegemonic country, but to hinder its actions—by increasing its costs" (Romero and Corrales, Pg. 219).

Even the most damaging action President Chavez could take in this realm is not possible for "structural reasons alone", which Romero and Corrales believe are "vacuous" and include "Chavez's threats of cutting off the oil supply to the United States"; because "without US oil trade, Chavez would have to sacrifice the (his) Bolivarian Revolution" (Romero and Corrales, Pg. 238). More importantly, Romero and Corrales demonstrate that "Chavez has few incentives to suddenly come out as a pro-US world leader" due to the fact that "he gains (a lot) by maintaining a certain degree of political conflict with the US as long as economic relations remain intact" (Romero and Corrales, Pg. 242).

Therefore, aside from the "anti-American" issue that was hyped up in the media following the CELAC Summit in Caracas (i.e. regarding the lack of participation of the USA and CELAC's potential to replace the OAS), what were the reasons behind the celebration and creation of CELAC? There are several reasons depending upon which one of the thirty-three CELAC countries you ask, however, there are most likely three important and timely reasons in general.

The first reason relates to the coup d'état that took place in Honduras in 2009. Alex Main claims that the "idea of CELAC (…) was first hatched in the wake of the US' unilateral decision to support elections held under a de facto government in Honduras despite the opposition of nearly every other country in the hemisphere (Main). He explained "prior to these elections, attempts were made to pass resolutions within the OAS rejecting elections under the coup regime, but the US thwarted these attempts at every turn" highlighting the important fact that "for many Latin American governments, the Honduras experience confirmed that the OAS was not a space in which sensitive political crises could be resolved" (Main).

The second reason the CELAC was created could be attributed to an "accumulation of factors", which have accrued over the last six decades. For example, the Honduras experience confirming that the OAS was not a space in which sensitive political crises could be solved, was not a first for the OAS. Many Latin American countries have viewed the OAS as a pawn of the US Government since its Charter was created in 1948 ("OEA"). Not to mention, the OAS during the Cold War era served as a justification for direct or indirect US intervention into countries throughout the hemisphere. For example, between 1946 and 2006, there were almost sixty coup d'états or attempted coup d'états worldwide with 24 percent of them having occurred in the Americas (Human Security Report Project). Selected US interventions, both direct (US military and CIA activity that changed governments) and indirect (government regime changes in which the US was decisive) in Latin America alone, during this same time period, amounted to approximately thirtyseven (Coatsworth). In February 2010, as a result of the Summit of Unity in Mexico, and its proposal to create CELAC, Bolivian president Evo Morales said that "he saw the new (CELAC) group as a way for the region to advance without the 'control, blackmail, and attempted coups' that he says have characterized the US' participation in the region" ("The Latin Americanist").

For instance, on September 25, 1963, Dominican president Juan Bosch was overthrown by a coup d'état led by a military junta (Gleijeses Pg. 106). This coup d'état was the result of internal disagreements and socioeconomic conflicts among different sectors of Dominican society, all of which are frequently common in a democratic transition, especially from dictatorship—as was the case in the Dominican Republic at the time. The dictatorship left misery, suffering, and inequality; and the "combination of inequality and democracy tends to cause a movement to the left everywhere" (Castañeda, Pg. 30). The Bosch Presidency was democratically elected with over 58 percent of the vote, while his election came on the heels of the tyrannical thirty-one year dictatorship of General Rafael L. Trujillo, whose reign ended in his chaotic murder in 1961 (Gleijeses Pg. 86). The US played a decisive role, not only in the death of General Trujillo, but also in the overthrow of President Bosch.

Gleijeses points out that there was "no proof" that "American military attachés—either on their own orders or on orders from the Pentagon—ever incited Dominican officers to overthrow Bosch", however, he cautions that "such a thesis is not impossible" (Gleijeses Pg. 98). Gleijeses, however, does demonstrate that "at least one American diplomat (at the time) worked overtly to overthrow Bosch" (Gleijeses Pg. 98). He highlighted how "Fred Somerford, a labor attaché with the American Embassy in Santo Domingo, and boss of the powerful labor federation CONATRAL, which was created, supported, and financed by the US (…) became (Somerford's) weapon against the president (Bosch)" (Gleijeses Pg. 98). The CONATRAL Federation also publicly criticized President Bosch for "not suppressing the Communists" and requested publicly that the (Dominican) military "to oust the President" (Gleijeses Pg. 98).

It was confirmed that then US Ambassador John Bartlow Martin had said in September of 1963, "Christian Manifestations have run their course, we had known that the general strike (in the Dominican Republic) might be the cívicos ultimate weapon. They would try to shut down both Santo Domingo and Santiago. Labor unions might join. If they could keep cities shut down for two or three days, tension would get screwed tight, and rioting might start. Troops must quell riots" (Gleijeses Pg. 105). This statement contributed to evidence of the US' interest in covering up the coup d'état by having the troops simultaneously quell the riots while purging "the Presidential Palace of an inept incumbent" demonstrating that it was "less a coup d'état than an indispensable surgical excision, demanded by an exasperated people (Gleijeses Pg. 105). Although President Bosch won the elections by an overwhelming majority in December of 1962, Thomas C. Mann, then US Assistant Secretary of State for Inter-American Affairs mentioned on record at the White House that Juan Bosch was "not qualified to govern" (Vega, Pg. 21).

After the coup d'état led by a military junta in 1963, the Dominican Republic remained plagued by increasing political instability, military infighting, social struggle, and ineffective governance. The country ended up having a civil war (Chester, Pg. 55). The fighting was between factions that supported the return to power of its democratically-elected president Juan Bosch, led by Coronel Francisco A. Caamaño; and forces of the military junta led by General Elías Wessin y Wessin (Chester, Pg. 54). As the side of Caamaño (supporting Juan Bosch) began to gain ground in the fight, the US Administration of President Lyndon B. Johnson began to grow leery and fearful of Communists and Communist supporters gaining a foothold in the Dominican Republic. There was no public mention of a "Communist threat" initially, but the US Government intervened in the Dominican Republic anyway on the evening of April 28, 1965, with President Johnson announcing "that the US had been informed by military authorities in the Dominican Republic that American lives were in danger (...) and that these authorities were no longer able to guarantee their safety" (Gleijeses Pg. 256).

Thereafter, what began as an humanitarian mission in rescue of American citizens with a total of 536 US troops, turned into 1,166 US troops because "there (were) signs that people trained outside the Dominican Republic (were) seeking to gain control", to finally over 23,000 US troops in the Dominican Republic—almost half the amount of US troops serving in the Vietnam War during the same period (Gleijeses Pg. 256-258). Throughout the US intervention, President Johnson utilized the OAS as a tool for justifying the US presence in the Dominican Republic, as was done in the other US interventions throughout the Western Hemisphere during the decades leading up to the end of the Cold War. On April 30, 1965, President Johnson stated "it is very important that representatives of the OAS be sent to the Dominican Republic, just as soon as they can be sent there (…) loss of time may mean that it is too late to preserve freedom, which alone can lead to the establishment of true democracy (…) this, I am sure, is what the people of the Dominican Republic want (…) late action, or delay in a such a case could mean a failure to accomplish the agreed objectives of the American states" (i.e. OAS) (US Department of State, Pg. 23).

Therefore, as a result of the OAS having been: one, utilized as a tool or pawn of the US Government during the case of US intervention in the Dominican Republic in 1965; or two, dominated by the US in instances including the aftermath of the coup d'état in Honduras in 2009; or, three, manipulated by the US in countless other examples throughout past decades; all together contribute to these factors leading to a more conducive political environment for Latin American and Caribbean to create an alternative to the OAS (i.e. CELAC). Also, these factors and the evidence behind the aforementioned reasons help to demonstrate that CELAC is not a question of "anti" or "pro" American, especially in the case of its creation. The aforementioned reasons, up until this point, reveal that the thirty-three CELAC member countries' motivation is based more upon their need for a regional organization that works for their interests and helps to solve their problems in this current increasingly dynamic, global and interdependent world. The CELAC members increasingly see the OAS as "an historical anachronism, harkening back to a time when the US exercised much more direct influence in the region's affairs" (Main).

Taking that final point into consideration, the third reason that CELAC was created deals with issues related to economic globalization, neoliberalization, and the failure of the Washington Consensus to produce sufficient results for Latin American and Caribbean countries throughout the 1990s. Levitsky and Roberts address that although the "free market model (of the Washington Consensus) succeeded in controlling inflation"; in much of the Latin America, however, "it (the model) was plagued by anemic growth, periodic financial crises, and a deepening of social and economic inequalities" (Levitsky and Roberts, Pg. 2). Although Latin America is "no longer defined by a commitment to a socialist model of development", all countries are "committed to a more equitable growth model", while some countries are increasingly "more willing than others to break with neoliberal orthodoxy (by using state power to regulate markets, alter property relations, and redistribute income)" (Levitsky and Roberts, Pg. 3).

Taylor explains how one of CELAC's key features is "a collective desire to increase regional "solidarity and social inclusion" while enhancing "complementarity between the region's economies" (Taylor). He highlighted how CELAC's members are "trying to figure out ways their economies can complement each other, rather than following the strict path of competitive economic relations", while emphasizing that "its not just Bolivia and Ecuador (or Venezuela) that are trying to push a social agenda", but "governments, regardless of whether they lean right or left, are giving more priority to addressing the symptoms and the causes of poverty (...) as well as making a priority of a social agenda that was for so long undermined, even marginalized during the phase of neoliberalism" (i.e. Washington Consensus in the 1990s) (Taylor). Chilean president Piñera underlined the fact that within CELAC there are (political) "differences of opinion", but he stated "vive la difference"; and in his capacity as the 2012 President of CELAC, he called upon all Member States to be guided by "the principles of liberty, democracy, respect for human rights, and justice", and above all, their "deep love of the people" ("LAC Summit Ends with Founding of CELAC"). President Piñera also asked CELAC's members to "join forces and make quality education possible" and to scale-up the "fight against poverty" with "multiple investments in science and technology" (Ebeling).

It has been acknowledged that the US economy alone is "equal to that of all other countries in the region combined" and "relations and trade agreements have long been dominated by US (economic) policy" (Taylor). In this respect, the CELAC Member States addressed the effects of the international financial crisis, which was born in the US, and exported throughout the global financial system and economy due to the increasingly global and integrated nature of financial markets.

Harnecker shows that this third reason for the creation of the CELAC demonstrates the "end of the cycle of anti-imperialist revolutions" and the necessity to prioritize, what she calls "anti-neoliberal struggles, as opposed to anti-imperialist or anti-capitalist (struggles)" as have existed in the past (Harnecker Pg. 142). She believes that the "information revolution" has contributed to the ability of "capital today (...) to function as a single unit in real time on a planetary scale" where "massive sums of money are transferred in seconds by electronic circuits that unite the financial world (...) made possible (...) thanks to the new infrastructure generated by information and communication technology (Harnecker Pg. 143144). These technologies and the capital behind them (as well as the capital that flows across their circuits) are dominated by the US.

Harnecker expresses concern for the challenge posed by the "current unipolar world" dominated by the US—a country that "coined the term globalization" according to her; versus "the bipolar world that existed at the time of the triumph of the Cuban Revolution" (Harnecker, Pg. 144145). Harnecker expounded upon her concern by stating that "it (is) not the same to act in a world in which workers had much more power of negotiation due to their capacity to paralyze production" than it is to act in a world where "capital can immediately respond to any salary or tax increase by moving to a more promising country (...) putting great emphasis on programs of social development (...) as a result of an enormous amount of capital pull(ing) out" (Harnecker, Pg. 145). She echoed Noam Chomsky's reference to these forces as a type of "virtual senate of financial speculators" who can vote instantaneously against "social development policies by withdrawing enormous sums of capital from (a) country, with disastrous consequences" (Harnecker, Pg. 145). Multiple countries at CELAC's Summit in Caracas referred to the effects of financial speculators on their economies, particularly when discussing the effects of the international financial crisis and the booms and busts commodity prices took (and continue to take) as a dimension of the said crisis.

Because of effects of globalization today—both the opportunities, but more so, the challenges—Latin America is obligated to join together to collectively confront the same challenges (and opportunities). As a result of globalization, the role of the State (in national development) needs to be rethought (continuously)— especially for smaller Latin American and Caribbean States, particularly due to the fact that economic superpowers such as the US, and increasingly China; as well as multinational corporations and large investment banks and financial institutions, with global reach; hold the cards regarding future economic stability and well being of Latin America. CELAC stands to help Latin America and the Caribbean leverage the global economy.

In the 1990's, nearly "all governments of the region embraced the Washington Consensus philosophy of free markets, deregulation, privatization and the downsizing of the state and its role in the economy" (Main). In the early 2000's there was an overwhelming rejection for these neoliberal policies; and, as a result "the election of left-of-center governments" took place throughout the region (Main). These same elected governments benefited from the "post-2002 global commodities boom"; and, as a result, "Latin America averaged 5.5 percent growth per year between 2004 and 2007 (Levitsky and Roberts, Pg. 10). Due to this economic progress, the same center-left governments were reelected including: Brazil (2006, 2010), Chile (2006), Venezuela (2006), Argentina (2007), Bolivia (2009), Ecuador (2009), and Uruguay (2009), thereby extending the so-called shift to the left in the region (Levitsky and Roberts, Pg. 10).

It could also be quite possibly true, that these governments, as a result of the 2008 commodities boom, perceive CELAC as an opportunity to "buy some insurance" for their economies by: one, looking inward to their own region; two, avoiding the mammoth US economy to the North (that currently struggles with economic recovery and) that created the global financial and economic crisis (which is primarily responsible for the financial speculation in commodities markets that burst the financial bubble that kept commodity prices high; and respective economic growth levels in the commodity exporting economies of Latin America); and three, while diversifying their economies (which are dominated by commodity exports to China and other emerging economies) by complementing them with other economic opportunities throughout the Latin American region.

This leads to the second precept, which has guided and dominated Inter-American relations, that being that foreign government regimes (i.e. CELAC members) or regional entities (i.e. CELAC itself) are often deemed of the "left". Castañeda believes there is not one "left" today, rather there are two "lefts"; the first representing a "modern, open-minded, reformist, and internationalist" that "springs paradoxically, from the hardcore left of the past"; while the other "born of the great tradition of Latin American populism, is nationalist, strident, and close-minded (Castañeda, Pg. 29). He states that the first is well aware of its past mistakes (as well as those of its erstwhile role models in Cuba and the Soviet Union)", while the "second, unfortunately has not" (Castañeda, Pg. 29). Harnecker defines the "left" as the "convergences of all the forces that stand up against the capitalist system with its profit logic, which fight for an alternative society based on humanism and solidarity and built upon the interests of the working classes, freeing them from material poverty and the spiritual misery, which is bred by capitalism" (Harnecker, Pg. 143).

Throughout the Cold War era, the most extreme form of "left" could quite possibly be "Communism". The US Government during the Johnson Administration never clearly and publicly came out and deemed Juan Bosch a "Communist", however, there were implications that socialists (leftists) were over-running his political party and could possibly turn the Dominican Republic into the next Castroist-style communist Cuba. On April 30, 1965, just two days after the beginning of the US intervention in the Dominican Republic, "Johnson gave the public first glimpse of the real nature of the 'humanitarian intervention'"(Gleijeses, Pg. 258). Shortly two days thereafter, President Johnson took up the theme again, although this time, with increased vigor stating, "Communist leaders, many of them trained in Cuba, seeing a chance to increase disorder, to gain a foothold, joined the revolution" (Gleijeses, Pg. 258). Four days later on May 8, 1965, US Secretary of State Dean Rusk stated, "What began in the Dominican Republic as a democratic revolution was taken over by Communist conspirators who had been trained for, and had carefully planned, that operation. Had they succeeded in establishing a government, the Communist seizure of power would in all likelihood have been irreversible, thus frustrating the declared principles of the OAS" (US Department of State, Pg. 20).

Part of the problem was that Juan Bosch was elected president of the Dominican Republic just three short months after the Cuban Missile Crisis took place (Vega, Pg. 19). This dangerous standoff between the nuclear powers of the US and the then Union of Soviet Socialist Republics (USSR) was an occurrence of planetary proportions. The world came to the brink of nuclear war, and possibly nuclear annihilation, as a result of the tensions that cultivated between these two countries that dominated the Cold War era. It was almost as if the US was increasingly blinded by its "anti-Communist" agenda and policies. It seems it failed to understand true democracy. Even US President John F. Kennedy remarked about the trauma the Cuban Missile Crisis had caused for his staff (i.e. ExComm), to such an extent that he shared with his counselor Ted Sorensen that he thought Secretary of State Rusk had "overworked himself to the point of mental and physical exhaustion" (Sorensen, Pg. 287). And Secretary of State Rusk was one of the primary US Government officials fueling the anti-Communist agenda and sentiments regarding the Dominican Republic during the US intervention. He misunderstood Dominican Republic for Cuba; two different countries, perhaps, because of his own personal traumatizing experience with the Cuban Missile Crisis.

President Juan Bosch was not communist. He was a social democrat. Juan Bosch also believed in capitalism and the market as a pillar to a thriving democracy. President Bosch's problem was that he began to reassert his "nation's sovereignty", "he angered US officials by failing to mention the US's Alliance for Progress (with the region)" during his presidential inauguration ceremony of which then US Vice-President Lyndon B. Johnson attended (Gleijeses, Pg. 95). Juan Bosch also had problems because he expressed desire to "secure aid from sources other than the US", he denounced a previous contract the country had with "the American firm Thomas A. Pappas and Associates claiming that Dominican interests had been grossly flouted", his "plans for social reforms earned him the enmity of American business interests in Santo Domingo"; and, according to US Ambassador Martin "he showed a surprising tolerance" and an "astonishing passivity vis-à-vis the Dominican communists" (Gleijeses, Pg. 96). As a democrat, Juan Bosch's intention was to appease all sectors and societal interests and to respect their ideology, beliefs, religions, and values. Eventually, however, even those on the "left" were opposing him; and the lack of US support for Bosch created a vicious circle that incited vigor in them (and other sectors) to emerge in further opposition to the new Dominican president.

Unfortunately, Juan Bosch, during the time of his overthrow and his country's civil war was wrongfully judged for who he allegedly was. Juan Bosch would have fared better, if he were judged rightfully; and more so, for who he was not, rather than who he was perceived to be. For example, President Bosch was not "anti-American". President Bosch was not "Communist". President Bosch was not willing to appease special interests at the cost of the Dominican people as a whole. Juan Bosch was a democrat, who believed in democratic values and social justice for his citizens. Unfortunately, for this, he paid a price. Perhaps, if he had had the backing of one of the two superpowers in the bipolar world of the Cold War era (as the neighboring Caribbean island of Cuba had) he would have fared differently.

Perhaps Juan Bosch's time came too early. The 1960's were a difficult time for democratic transitions, especially for those in the region, and more so for the Caribbean during a moment when the USSR and US confronted each other with communist Cuba serving as a USSR proxy. Today, in the sprit of democracy, Juan Bosch would fit right in with the social democratic transformation underway in the Latin American and Caribbean region. Nearly two-thirds of Latin America lives under some form of leftlearning national government; and now, as opposed to before, democracy has played a role in empowering the left of the region to govern with political stability (Levitsky and Roberts, Pg. 2). This modern day transformation has become a "paradigm shift that has transformed policymaking in nearly every country of the region, even with right-leaning governments" as they too adopt "social agendas" that address the needs of the poor (Main).

Therefore, CELAC's strongest quality seems to be the fact that it is united by its diversity and its vision for Simon Bolivar's dream. No part of CELAC is considered a quality because of a few countries that pretend to lead (or portray that they are) the frontrunner of the group—particularly speaking frankly of those of whom lean further to the left than others (some all the way to Communism, such as Cuba). The most important aspect of CELAC is its universal nature, where no country, including those that represent what Castañeda calls "the second left", has enough regional clout or political capital to stand in the way of its universality.

Consequently, Inter-American relations will continue to remain interesting and will continue to transform themselves; and, the US should not make the same mistake it made yesterday with President Juan Bosch. It should not formulate a policy with one country (i.e. 1963 Dominican Republic), based upon its policy with ano ther (i.e. 1963 Cuba). Taking that approach today, in the era of CELAC, would be another mistake. It would not be prudent for modern day US policy in the region.

BIBLIOGRAPHY

Castañeda, Jorge G. "Latin America's Left Turn." Foreign Affairs. Volume 85, Number 3 (May-June 2006): 2843.

Chester, Eric Thomas. Rag-Tags, Scum, Riff-Raff and Commies: The U.S. Intervention in the Dominican Republic, 19651966. New York, New York: Monthly Review Press, 2001.

Coatsworth, John. "US Latin American Relations: World War II to the Present" Lecture. School of International and Public Affairs (SIPA). Columbia University, New York, New York. 19 September 2011.

"Comunidad de Estados Latinoamericanos y Caribeños (CELAC)." Ministerio de Relaciones Exteriores de Venezuela. 03 December 2011. <www.celac.gob.ve>

"Cumbre de la Unidad de América Latina y el Caribe." Secretaría de Relaciones Exteriores de los Estados Unidos de México. 23 February 2011. <www.sre.gob.mx/cumbredelaunidad/default.htm>

Ebeling Jr., Paul A. "Latin America Comes of Age with CELAC." Live Trading News. 10 December 2011. Ebeling Heffernan. <www.livetradingnews.com/latinamericacomesofagewithcelac59410.htm>

Gleijeses, Piero. The Dominican Crisis, The 1965 Constitutionalist Revolt and American Intervention. Baltimore and London: The Johns Hopkins University Press, 1978.

Harnecker, Marta. "On Leftist Strategy." Journal of Science & Society, Vol. 69 (April 2005); 142-152.

"History of the Organization of American States (OAS)." Organización de Estados Americanos (OEA)." 03 December 2011. <www.oas.org/en/about /our_history.asp>

Human Security Report Project. Human Security Brief 2007. Vancouver: HSRP, 2008. <www.hsrgroup.org/docs/Publications/ HSB2007/Figures/2007HSBrief_ fig3_8CoupsDEtat.jpg> <www.hsrgroup.org/docs/Publications/HSB2007/Figures/2007HSBrief_ fig3_9CoupsDEtatByRegion.jpg>

Keller, Mark. "Latin American Leaders Converge to Form CELAC." Americas Society & Council of the Americas (AS/COA). New York, New York, USA. 02 December 2011. <www.ascoa.org/articles/3825/ Latin_American_Leaders_ Converge_to_Form_CELAC>

"Latin American and Caribbean Summit Ends with Founding of CELAC." Latin American Herald Tribune. Caracas, Venezuela. 03 December 2011. <http://www.laht.com/article.asp?ArticleId=44 9373&CategoryId=10718>

Levitsky, Steven, and Kenneth M. Roberts. The Resurgence of the Latin American Left. Baltimore and London: The Johns Hopkins University Press, 2011.

Main, Alex. "CELAC: Speaking for Latin America and the Caribbean." The Center for Economic and Policy Research (CEPR) Blog. 06 December 2011. <www.cepr.net/index.php/blogs/ ceprblog/celacspeakingforlatinamericaandthecaribbean>

"Mujica calls CELAC 'a second independence' but warns beware of dogmatism." MercoPress. 05 December 2011. <http:// en.mercopress.com/2011/12/ 05/mujicacallscelacasecond independencebutwarnsbewareofdogmatism>

Oppenheimer, Andres. "New Latin American group will have no teeth". Miami Herald. Miami, Florida, USA. 04 December 2011. <www.miamiherald.com /2011/12/03/2529070/ newlatinamericangroupwill.html>

Padgett, Tim. "Latin America's CELAC Summit: A Definitive Rejection of the U.S.?" Time.com World. Mexico City, Mexico. 02 December 2011.

<http://globalspin.blogs.time.com/2011/12/02/latinamerica scelacsummitadefinitiverejectionoftheus/>

Romero, Carlos, and Javier Corrales. "Relations between the United States and Venezuela, 20012009, A Bridge in Need of Repairs." Contemporary U.S.Latin American Relations: Cooperation or Conflict in the 21st Century? (Contemporary Inter-American Relations). Eds. Jorge I. Dominguez and Rafael Fernandez de Castro. London: Routledge, 2010. 217-246.

Royster, Michael. "The Curmudgeon on CELAC." The Rio Times News. Rio De Janiero, Brazil. 06 December 2011. <http://riotimesonline.com/brazilnews/opinioneditorial/opinion/thecurmudgeononcelac/>

Rueda, Jorge. "Leaders at Americas talks: world economy top worry." Associated Press. 03 December 2011. <www.ap.org>

Sorensen, Ted. Counselor: A Life at the Edge of History. New York, New York: Harper, 2008.

Taylor, Guy. "CELAC Signals Start of a New Era in Latin America." World Politics Review. 05 May 2011. <www.worldpoliticsreview.com/trendlines/8750/celacsignalsstartofanewerainlatinamerica)

United States Department of State (DOS). The Dominican Crisis: The Hemisphere Acts, Official Statements of President Lyndon B. Johnson, Secretary of State Dean Rusk, and Ellsworth Bunker. Washington DC: US Department of State, 1965.

Vega, Bernardo. El Peligro Comunista en la Revolución de Abril, ¿Mito o Realidad? Santo Domingo, Dominican Republic: Fundación Cultural Dominicana, 2006.

"Yanqui Go Home?" The Latin Americanist Blog. 22 February 2010. <http://ourlatinamerica.blogspot.com/2010/02/yanquigohome.html>

www.ingramcontent.com/pod-product-compliance
Lightning Source LLC
Chambersburg PA
CBHW031049180526
45163CB00002BA/750